Teachers' Classroom Decision-Making

Teachers' Classroom Decision-Making

James Calderhead
University of Lancaster

HOLT, RINEHART AND WINSTON
London · New York · Sydney · Toronto

Holt, Rinehart and Winston Ltd: 1 St Anne's Road
Eastbourne, East Sussex BN21 3UN

British Library Cataloguing in Publication Data

Calderhead, James
  Teachers' classroom decision-making.
  1. Classroom management—Decision making
  I. Title
  371.1'02   LB3013
ISBN 0–03–910513–X

Printed and bound in Great Britain
by Billing & Sons Limited, Worcester.

Last digit is print number: 9 8 7 6 5 4 3 2 1

Acknowledgements

The author is grateful to the following for permission to reproduce copyright material: the American Educational Research Association for the figure on p. 9 from Peterson, P.L. & Clark, C.M. 'Teachers' reports of their cognitive processes during teaching', *American Educational Research Journal*, 15(4), 555–65; David Hargreaves, Stephen Hester and Frank Mellor for the extract on pp. 29–30, taken from Hargreaves, D.H., Hester, S.K. & Mellor, F.J. *Deviance in Classrooms*, London: Routledge and Kegan Paul, 1975; and Ian Bliss of St. Martin's College, Lancaster for the transcript on p. 101.

Preface

THIS book is about the decisions teachers make in day-to-day classroom life. In organising instruction, managing the class, and in dealing with the many and varied demands encountered during the course of the school day, teachers engage in much thinking and decision-making. However, these mental aspects of teaching are often taken for granted. It is unusual, for example, to find decision-making entering into the professional discussions of teachers, or becoming the focus of attention in teacher training, although decision-making frequently is a matter of deep concern to beginning teachers.

Similarly, it is only quite recently that researchers, from various backgrounds, have been attracted to the study of teachers' thoughts and decisions. However, the literature in this field is now steadily growing and reflects a variety of interests and perspectives. Psychologists, for example, have investigated the nature of teachers' thinking and its relationship to classroom interaction. Sociologists have explored how teachers' decisions are influenced by institutional and societal pressures. Curriculum researchers have studied how teachers' thinking about the curriculum mediates its translation into practice.

The aim of this book is to bring together this wide range of research, and to relate it to teachers' everyday experiences, in the belief that research can be of value to teachers, helping them to understand and further develop their own classroom practice. Although the book is intended primarily for teachers and students in training, in either primary or secondary schools, it is hoped that others concerned with teaching may also find it of interest. The exercises concluding each chapter are intended to help students relate the material to their own experiences in classrooms. These exercises might also form the basis of tutorial activities, benefiting from discussion with tutors and other students and might be adapted or extended by tutors to suit particular course requirements.

J. CALDERHEAD

Contents

1

Introduction: The Teacher as Decision-Maker

DECISION, THOUGHT AND ACTION

WE each perceive our environment in a unique and individual way. Surrounded by myriad cues – sights, sounds, sensations – we select and interpret those which convey meaning and significance. We develop ways of perceiving and interpreting that enable us to understand and make sense of the environment. In so doing, we learn to anticipate events and predict their future courses. We identify situations where our actions may be influential and judge the possible effects of alternative strategies. Our understanding leads us to identify choices and make decisions.

Consider, for example, our social interactions. In everyday life, we meet a variety of people. Some we might perceive as friendly and supportive, others as hostile or aggressive. We know from our discussions with others that a person can be perceived quite differently by different people. However, it is our own assessment of a person that determines how we expect them to behave, how we interact with them – what we say and do – and how we expect them to respond to ourselves.

Our decisions provide bridges between thought and action, linking the ways in which we understand the environment with our actions in it. But precisely what does the process of decision-making involve? What do we do when we make decisions? It is difficult to find any one account of decision-making which is both detailed and realistic. Models of decision-making frequently outline stages of the process (such as identifying alternatives and predicting the consequences of each) but often depict decision-making as a very rational, sequential activity and do not adequately represent the real-life mental experiences involved. Consideration of some of our own decisions can serve to demonstrate that we engage in different types of decision-making and that our thoughts commonly guide our actions in a variety of ways.

Reflective decisions

Some decisions do involve much thinking and evaluation. Deciding upon a career, for example, typically involves considering various possible occupations, acquiring information about them, imagining oneself in different occupational roles and comparing and contrasting their attractions. These deliberations eventually lead to particular career preferences, which then determine a number of future actions. Important decisions which can be taken over a period of time are frequently reflective, involving the identification of alternatives and the prediction and evaluation of their outcomes.

Immediate decisions

On other occasions, our actions depend upon more immediate thinking. If, while crossing a road we notice a bus travelling towards us at high speed, we do not pause to ponder the alternatives! Many everyday actions in fact depend upon snap judgements or quick intuitive decision-making. Based on our understanding of the situation we confront, we make a hasty guess at an appropriate response. Evaluation of alternatives is unlikely to occur before the action, though it may occur afterwards, particularly if our action leads to an unsatisfactory outcome. This then better prepares us for future events of a similar kind.

Routine decisions

Some decisions in everyday life are made so often that they have become automatic and routine. In first learning to drive a car, many decisions have to be made – decisions to change gear, to accelerate or slow down, decisions concerning how to direct the car safely and how to cope with various unexpected events, etc. Once experienced in driving, however, these decisions are made automatically and the task of driving becomes largely routine. Many everyday social interactions also involve routine decision-making. In meeting familiar people in familiar contexts, our actions are guided by a set of well-established routines. We become most aware of this when we meet strangers in an unfamiliar setting, an occasion on which we reflect more consciously about our social behaviour.

Real-life decisions, whether reflective, immediate or routine, are made within a context of influences and constraints. Factors beyond our control may limit the options available to us or determine how we perceive these options. On some occasions these factors can be sufficiently powerful that decisions actually involve little scope for choice. The decision to go to school or college, to get a job, and even in some cases, decisions concerning the selection of a particular occupation, may be tightly constrained. Certainly there may be some intrinsic satisfactions in work or education, but these decisions are also influenced by social pressures (the expectations that parents, peers, teachers, husbands or wives have for us), legal regulations (the laws of our society and of institutions within it that penalise non-attendance at school and work), financial interdependencies (educational qualifications may determine our personal income which in turn determines our potential to do and buy the things we would like) and physical constraints (job availability). To decide not to work or be educated, given the opportunity, would for most people lead to clearly undesirable consequences. The society in which we live is in fact so organised as to weight the options available to us strongly in favour of one outcome.

Studies of decision-making focus upon the origins of human action. People's actions can often be puzzling and difficult to understand. Yet once aware of the thinking which preceded an action and the context in which that thinking developed, even astonishing acts of daring, violence or crime can become comprehensible. Investigations of decision-making help us to understand the actions of others and to appreciate how our own actions emerge from the thoughts and experiences we have and the context in which we live.

TEACHING DECISIONS

Schools and classrooms are complex environments in which teachers are called upon to play an active, central part. In order to carry out their professional function, and interact meaningfully with pupils and colleagues, they must develop ways of understanding this environment that enable them to make decisions, and guide their everyday actions.

Teachers' decisions again vary in their nature. Some are reflective. Decisions concerning the selection of appropriate teaching methods and curriculum content may be made over a fairly long period of time, require consultation with other staff, and involve considerable thought and evaluation. Other decisions are immediate. In the classroom, teachers meet a variety of unexpected situations: lessons don't go as well as expected, children experience unforeseen difficulties, the activities of the class are interrupted by sudden events. Such situations demand immediate and appropriate responses in order to minimise classroom disruption, pupils' loss of interest and failure to learn. Still other decisions have become such a common aspect of classroom practice that they are made automatically. In coping with the recurrent problems of classroom life, such as excessive noise, children finishing their work at different times or the need to provide feedback on pupils' performance rapidly, teachers employ a repertoire of established teaching routines. During periods of intensive interpersonal interaction, teachers may be heavily reliant upon these routines.

The terms *preactive* and *interactive* originally proposed by Jackson (1968) are often used to distinguish two contexts of teacher activity which are characterised by different types of decision-making. In the preactive phase, before lessons begin or at the end of the school day when the children have gone home, teachers are involved in planning and evaluation, processes which require them to make reflective decisions of a problem-solving nature. In the interactive phase, when teachers are in face-to-face interaction with their pupils, events generally come and go too rapidly to permit such reflection, and teachers must rely upon immediate, intuitive or routine decision-making.

Recent research on teachers' thinking has investigated the nature of decision-making in both the preactive and interactive phases and has supported and elaborated upon this distinction. Teachers' thinking in the preactive phase has been explored using a procedure known as *protocol analysis* (or *process tracing*) in which researchers require teachers to verbalise their normally covert thoughts while planning. In some studies, teachers have been trained to do this and are provided with an opportunity to practise making commentaries before these are finally tape-recorded for future analysis. Research on teachers' thinking during classroom interaction, on the other hand, has adopted *stimulated recall procedures* in which teachers' lessons are video-taped. The video-tape is replayed soon afterwards to teachers to help them recall their thoughts at the time, and thus stimulate a commentary on their past thinking. Again teachers have often been allowed to practise the procedure before the data are systematically collected and analysed.

Commentaries obtained through the use of protocol analysis or stimulated recall procedures may not be entirely complete or totally accurate accounts of teachers' real thoughts since there may be occasions when teachers cannot recall their thinking, may be reluctant to reveal it, or provide rationalisations for their behaviour rather than the thoughts they actually experienced. However, despite the shortcomings of commentaries and the uncertain status of some, they can at times provide valuable insights into the nature of teaching.

For example, Table 1.1 lists the comments made by a primary school teacher when viewing a video-tape of part of an arithmetic lesson with a class of 11-year-olds. The teacher was simply instructed to recall what she was thinking about at the time. The resulting commentary reveals the teacher's concern for checking whether individual children have understood or are using appropriate techniques, a concern for explaining a particular arithmetic process, a concern with the attention and involvement of the group (and the remainder of the class) in their respective activities and a concern with matching the difficulty of particular questions with the ability of the pupils. Such comments, though they are not very detailed reports of the teacher's actual thinking, help us to understand what the teacher was doing and the concerns that guided her actions at the time. Studies of teachers' thinking in both preactive and interactive phases of teaching help us to conceptualise the nature of teachers' practice.

Research on teachers' thoughts while planning (e.g. Morine 1976, Peterson, Marx and Clark 1978, Yinger 1980, McCutcheon 1980, Ben-Peretz 1981) reveals that teachers, in this context, think mostly about the construction of *activities* which specify how their own and pupils' time is to be occupied in the classroom. An *activity* defines what teacher and pupils will do. Lessons may consist of one activity (e.g. doing spelling) or of several activities occurring consecutively or at the same time. In the lesson described in Table 1.1, for example, the class is organised into groups and although they are all involved in arithmetic, each group is engaged in a separate activity, involving different work, taking different amounts of time, requiring different levels of help and supervision from the teacher.

Planning activities involves teachers in various decisions. They must decide the subject matter to be covered and perhaps how it is to be sequenced, the materials to be used, the pupils who are to be included in each activity, how the class is to be organised, possibly the time in the school day the activity will take place, and what the teacher will expect from the pupils in terms of both behaviour and achievement during the course of each activity. Decisions such as these occupy a large proportion of teachers' thoughts in the planning they do at various times in the day when not interacting with their pupils.

As teachers become more experienced, their familiarity with planning activities for similar groups of pupils in similar contexts may obviate the

Table 1.1 *A teacher's commentary on part of a lesson, stimulated by video-tape*

Context: A lesson on the conversion of percentages is being taught to a group of eight 11-year-old pupils standing in front of the blackboard. The others in the class are working quietly in their seats on textbook exercises.

The teacher started the group lesson with some discussion of what percentages were, when they were used and what they meant, relating percentages to newspaper headlines regarding pay rises and bank interest rates. Having established that a percentage is equivalent to a fraction with denominator 100, and after demonstrating some examples of percentages and equivalent fractions on the blackboard, the teacher asks the group to convert examples of percentages into fractions, choosing individual children to reply.

Events immediately preceding teacher's comments	*Teacher's comments*
The teacher asks, 'What do you think seven and a half per cent would be as a fraction?' Brief silence and three children hesitantly put up their hands. The teacher calls upon Michael who answers, 'Three-fortieths, ' and the teacher replies 'Good. How did you do it?'	'I wanted to see if they could work it out for themselves.'
Michael explains his method, which was to reason that as 5% equals one-twentieth, 2½% would equal one-fortieth, and therefore 7½% [3 × 2½%] equals three-fortieths. The teacher then says, 'Very good. What would happen though if I asked you to convert eleven and a half per cent?' Michael responds with a puzzled expression.	'I was thinking that his method was O.K. in that case, but wasn't going to be so easy using the same method in other cases.'
The teacher explains how to deal with half per cents by converting percentages into fractions with denominators of two hundred and cancelling down. Two examples are worked through on the blackboard.	'This was part of the lesson. I was explaining the method I wanted them to use.'
On turning round from the blackboard, the teacher calls the name of a child who is talking in another part of the classroom.	'I noticed Simon didn't seem to be getting on and had a lot to say.'
Giving some examples to be answered orally, the teacher asks, 'Seventeen and a half per cent: what's that as a fraction?' and waits for children to raise their hands.	'I was waiting until a few hands were raised to give the slower ones a chance to work it out.'
The teacher asks 'Twelve and half per cent: Charles?'	'He was absent yesterday. He had his hand up and I wanted to see if he'd cottoned on.'
The teacher asks, 'Thirty-seven and a half: Susan?'	'She didn't have her hand up. I thought she wasn't bothering.'

Table 1.1 *continued*

Events immediately preceding teacher's comments	Teacher's comments
The teacher says, 'What about twenty-two and a half per cent... Michael?'	'That was difficult. I thought the others might not be able to do it so I chose Michael.'

The teacher then directs pupils to a particular textbook exercise and sends them back to their seats.

necessity for many planning decisions. The experienced teacher may have come to assume certain characteristics of particular activities and developed a mental image of different types of lesson involving specific sequences of activities. The experienced teacher's planning may be partly routinised to the extent that planning a geography lesson on the life of a French farmer, for example, might centre largely around the recollection of how the lesson was taught on previous occasions, making some fine-tuning adjustments to this mental plan to allow for the different pupils and any different context, and making modifications suggested by previous experiences with the same or similar lessons. The teacher might have acquired additional materials and teaching aids on France, or could be talking to pupils who differ from those she or he taught previously, perhaps knowing nothing either of France or farming. The existing lesson plan would consequently be modified to suit the new context.

Research on teachers' thinking during classroom interaction, on the other hand, confirms that in this area of teachers' practice most decisions are immediate or routine. Mackay and Marland (1978) found that a group of American primary school teachers made an average of only about six decisions, in the sense of choices amongst alternatives, per hour-long lesson. In these there was little opportunity for reflection, teachers rarely considered any more than one alternative and spent little time in evaluation. Most of teachers' thinking in the classroom has been found to concern the implementation of previously planned activities (Mackay and Marland 1978, Peterson and Clark 1978, McNair and Joyce 1979). Teachers think mostly about what they have just done and what they are about to do next, as they engage in a process of translating mental plans into classroom practice. Decisions in the classroom generally occur only when something unexpected happens – the lesson is interrupted or the activities once implemented fail to run as smoothly as anticipated. At such times, teachers' thoughts often focus upon their pupils, considering why they do not understand or why they are inattentive, for instance, and teachers use the resulting judgements about pupils to decide how best to cope with the remainder of the lesson. Consequently, once classroom activities are established, much of the teachers' time may be taken up with a monitoring process occasionally leading to decisions when the activities deviate unexpectedly. This process is well described in a simple model of interactive decision-making proposed by Peterson and Clark (1978) based on an earlier model by Snow (1972) – see Fig. 1.1. In this, teachers are viewed as constantly selecting and interpreting cues from the classroom environment. As suggested above, these cues might concern pupils' levels of attention, or be indicators of whether or not pupils are understanding the lesson content. If the cues go beyond a certain acceptable threshold, teachers have to decide whether there are alternative strategies available to them to enable the classroom situation to be brought back on course. Furthermore, if alternatives are available, teachers must then decide how they are to act. For example, if pupils appear to lose interest in an activity, the teacher may first of all decide whether this lack of interest is of a minor or serious nature. If it is ten minutes before the end of the school period or day, the waning of interest may be perceived as quite normal. If more serious, however, the teacher might then consider whether there are alternative actions available (e.g. to stop the activity and start another, to attempt to relate the activity more closely to the children's known interests, to provide an alternative activity for children to do if they wish, to discuss with the class why they are losing interest, to stress to the children the importance of what they are doing, etc.) and then decide which alternative to implement or whether no action at all might be a better, or at least less disruptive, strategy.

Peterson and Clark's model may represent many immediate classroom decisions quite adequately, particularly those arising from unexpected events or pupil reactions, but teachers' responses to classroom situations are frequently more automatic and routine. Many teachers' actions would seem to be carried out as a matter of course with little thinking involved. Teachers often engage in routine actions to establish and maintain an activity, or in response to particular difficulties. In the above instance where pupils lose interest, for example, a teacher, having frequently encountered such situations, may respond automatically with an encouraging statement and emphasise the importance of what they are doing without thought of an alternative response.

The nature of teaching routines is well illustrated in a recent study of infant teachers' reading lessons (Hoffman and Kugle 1982). Here it was found that when listening to children read, teachers would typically respond to children's hesitations and mispronunciations with one of four

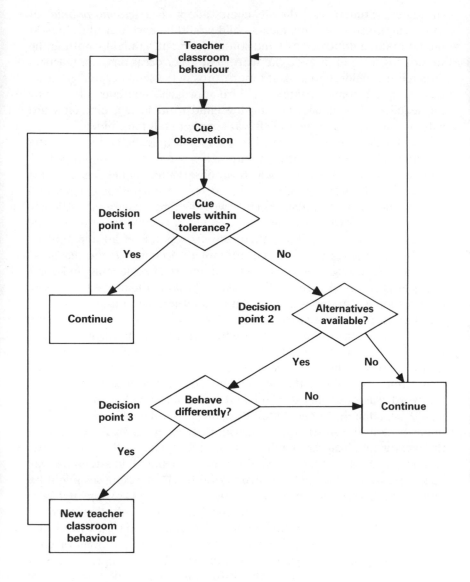

Fig. 1.1 *Peterson and Clark's (1978) model of interactive decision-making, representing the process of monitoring activities in the classroom.*

strategies. Sometimes, the teachers adopted a *grapho-phonic* or *sounding-out* strategy, in which a child would be encouraged to look at the letters of a difficult word and sound them out, gradually putting the sounds together to provide the word. On other occasions, the teachers directed the children to look at other words in the sentence and guess an unknown one from its context. A third approach sometimes adopted by the teachers was silence, leaving the child to identify a difficult word without any help, and the fourth was simply to tell the child.

The teachers were observed to respond quickly and apparently automatically in these four ways, but their reasons for responding with a particular strategy were not clear from observation alone. Sometimes a child's difficulty would receive a context response from the teacher and on other occasions a similar difficulty would be met with silence. Clearly one would not expect teachers to respond randomly in such circumstances, yet the rationale for their actions was not at all apparent to the observing researchers. In an attempt to account for the teachers' behaviour, the researchers video-taped the reading lessons and soon afterwards replayed them to the teachers, asking them to explain why they responded in one way rather than another. The reasons given by teachers varied considerably.

Some concerned the characteristics of *pupils*, particularly their reading ability; an able pupil, for instance, might be left to puzzle out a difficult word on his own because the teacher thought he could do it. Other reasons given by the teachers concerned the *materials* in use: if the word was unusually difficult and if the teacher thought the pupil would be unlikely to encounter it again in the near future, the child might be told it. On still other occasions, teachers' reasons referred to the *context* in which the reading activity took place: if the teacher was feeling particularly harassed at the time or if the child's reading was being assessed and formally recorded, the teachers' responses might be influenced. However, the majority of reasons given by the teachers concerned more than one single feature, and frequently their instructional reactions to hesitations and mispronunciations involved the operation of principles which took account of configurations of cues concerning pupils, materials *and* contexts. For example, teachers frequently reported ignoring the mispronunciations of lower-ability pupils if the error was relatively minor and if the pupil had already been interrupted for several other mispronunciations in the same reading activity, on the grounds that frequent interruptions could have a demoralising effect upon the child. Conversely, teachers also reported correcting the minor mispronunciations of higher-ability pupils when they were aware of having made few interruptions, on the grounds that the child would obtain some constructive feedback.

Hoffman and Kugle's research outlines a repertoire of routines employed by teachers in connection with one very specific teaching activity. Yet even in employing these few routines, it seems that teachers are capable of responding apparently automatically to quite complex configurations of cues, displaying some sensitivity to the abilities of the pupils, characteristics of the materials and context, and to the learning outcomes of the activity.

Hargreaves makes a similar observation in a study of secondary school teachers' reactions to indiscipline in the classroom (Hargreaves, Hester and Mellor 1975). Teachers were found to possess a large repertoire of reactions or 'treatments' which were automatically employed in response to finely discriminated configurations of cues concerning the pupil(s) involved, the situation and its context. The breaking of a test tube in a science lesson, for example, would receive one immediate response if it was broken during an experiment by a pupil believed by the teacher to be generally quiet and well-behaved, but quite another if it was broken during horseplay in the laboratory by a boy perceived to be disruptive and deviant.

Teachers' use of routines in teaching is probably an essential element of classroom survival. During the interactive phase of teaching, a primary school teacher typically engages in two or three hundred interactions each hour. Individual decisions concerning how to act, are, for most of these interactions, clearly impossible, and the teacher must rely on established routine practices. The rate of interaction for secondary school teachers is sometimes less, particularly where the teaching is fairly formal, but the demands placed upon teachers are still high.

Research on teachers' thinking in both the preactive and interactive phases informs us about the nature of teaching and the decision-making it involves. The research indicates that in the preactive phase the teacher makes decisions concerning the design and sequencing of activities that will appropriately occupy teacher and pupils during class time. In the interactive phase the teacher is engaged in implementing these activities and ensuring their successful completion, and in doing this the teacher may have to make several immediate decisions and rely upon a repertoire of teaching routines in order to cope with the demands of the classroom.

This description of teaching in terms of the planning, implementation and maintenance of activities, accurately reflects, for many teachers, their own teaching experiences. Certainly it is not difficult to find examples of teaching that conform to this. For example, well-organised, practical science lessons in secondary schools often follow a well-tried sequence of activities. They start with a class discussion directed by the teacher towards a consideration of a particular hypothesis and ways of testing it. This is followed by some practical work, perhaps carried out in groups, intended to test the initial hypothesis. A report-back session ensues, in which the class report and discuss their findings with the help of the teacher, and the lesson concludes with individual work where the pupils write up and comment on their experiment.

Similarly, creative writing lessons in the upper primary school generally follow a fairly stereotyped sequence of activities. The teacher first of all introduces a topic or stimulus (story, poem or interesting object) to the class. This is followed by a class discussion in which the teacher attempts to interest the pupils, seeks to elicit and clarify their ideas and generates appropriate vocabulary which may be listed on the blackboard. Finally, the teacher provides a series of reminders to the pupils about structuring their writing, or using appropriate punctuation, before encouraging them to write.

In fact, from one lesson to another, teachers appear to plan and establish familiar sequences of activities and cope routinely with a familiar range of classroom difficulties, interruptions and challenges. To think of teaching as the design, implementation and maintenance of activities, involving different types of decision-making, provides us with a way of understanding much of what teachers do.

CONSTRAINTS UPON TEACHER DECISION-MAKING

Teachers, however, are not the sole arbiters of their classroom practice. Just as our decisions in everyday life are sometimes tightly constrained, teachers' decisions in both the preactive and interactive phases of teaching occur within a context that can ultimately exert a powerful influence upon what happens in the classroom. *Physical* constraints such as the size and composition of the class and the materials available, and *ideological* constraints consisting of commonly held beliefs, values and expectations about the content and methods of teaching often determine what it is possible for teachers to do.

Many of these constraints are beyond the control of the individual teacher. Teachers cannot determine the size of their classes or the socioeconomic background of their pupils. They may also be relatively powerless to change the beliefs and expectations that headteachers, school governors, parents and perhaps even pupils hold for their professional conduct. In the case of secondary schools, the syllabus guidelines of the examination boards which largely determine the content of secondary education for older children, are similarly beyond teachers' individual control. Some of these constraints may be taken for granted by teachers who have grown accustomed to working within them. Some, such as a prescribed syllabus, may even be welcomed for the security they offer, relieving the teacher of the need to make certain decisions.

Owing to the powerful framework of physical and ideological constraints within which teachers work, their classroom practice may on occasion reflect the demands of that context more than teachers' own beliefs and convictions about good or appropriate teaching.

On other occasions, however, teachers may experience greater freedom to determine the nature of their practice, or may contribute to or negotiate the framework of constraints within which future decisions are made. For example, during the first few weeks of a new school year the teacher might be involved in decisions concerning the planning of the year's work, which in turn carry implications for what can be taught in individual lessons in the future. Similarly, the classroom work procedures and the norms for pupil behaviour that are established by the teacher early in the year will influence how the class functions in the coming months and determine the managerial and disciplinary decisions required of the teacher in the future.

To develop an understanding of teachers' classroom practice, of how it may be changed and improved, and of the capacity for teachers themselves to bring about such improvement, the study of teachers' thinking and decision-making must include investigation of the teaching context, the extent to which teachers are involved in establishing that context and the ways in which it limits or constrains teachers' thoughts, decisions and actions.

TEACHERS' DECISION-MAKING AND UNDERSTANDING EDUCATIONAL PRACTICE

Although we can observe teachers at work, engaging in a continuous flow and variety of actions and interactions, we cannot understand the real nature of teaching, and what it involves, from these observations alone.

For example, observational studies of classrooms have repeatedly found that teachers spend much of their time, in interacting with pupils, asking questions, obtaining responses from their pupils and in turn reacting to pupils' responses – a pattern of interaction commonly referred to as 'the recitation' (Hoetker and Ahlbrand 1969). Yet such observational reports obscure the nature of the teachers' task, since the intentions behind teachers' questions may vary considerably from one occasion to the next. A question may be asked of one child in order to redirect his wandering attention, that to another may be intended to boost her confidence by providing her with an opportunity to demonstrate her competence to the class. Questions may also be phrased in particular ways in order, for example, to stress a key item of information or to guide a child quickly to an appropriate answer. Similarly, Brophy (1981) describes the many functions that praise can fulfil within the classroom. When a teacher praises a pupil's response, it may, for example, be to signal to the rest of the class behaviour that the teacher expects, or to stress certain features of a child's reply or to re-establish a relationship with a pupil who has recently been reprimanded, communicating to the child that their contributions to the lesson are still valued.

To understand the nature of teaching and why teaching takes the form it does requires investigation of the thinking of teachers and the context in which this thinking occurs. Such an understanding of teaching is of value to many involved in education, particularly beginning teachers learning classroom skills, and to teachers and other educationalists interested in improving the quality of education.

DECISION-MAKING AND THE BEGINNING TEACHER

Learning to teach is a task fraught with difficulty. Student and probationer teachers often report being overwhelmed by their first few experiences in the classroom and they typically express concern about their own performance and competence as teachers (Fuller 1969, Taylor 1975). Many of their anxieties emerge from an uncertainty of how to cope with particular classroom situations, and a fear of being unable to deal with crises when they arise: what do I do if my planned lesson is completed very much more quickly than I expected? What do I do if they won't listen to me? Will I be able to cope?

Many of the beginning teacher's difficulties can be more fully understood when we consider the decision-making demands of teaching. Experienced teachers are able to plan and implement a wide variety of lessons quickly and easily, calling upon a memorised repertoire of regularly employed activities and using well-mastered routines to establish and maintain them. Beginning teachers, on the other hand, have to devote an enormous amount of time and thought to the development, organisation and sequencing of activities. They may have to think about the possible interests, abilities and behaviour characteristics of the pupils whom they have possibly never met before, and the implications these have for the lesson. They must become familiar with the materials available and the classroom context in which they will work. They may also surmise the expectations of the staff, parents and pupils with whom they will come into contact and consider how they will react to these. In addition beginning teachers must think about the techniques they will use to establish and maintain classroom activities, for although this is *routine* to the experienced teacher it may well require *conscious decisions* from the novice. For the beginning teacher there is clearly much to be learned and co-ordinated.

Some of the differences in the knowledge and thinking of experienced and beginning teachers are demonstrated in a study of teachers' reported strategies for coping with classroom incidents (Calderhead 1979). Three primary school teachers were asked to describe events which regularly occurred in their classrooms and to which they felt it would be important to respond. From these descriptions, a list of twenty-one 'critical incidents' was developed, including for example:

The class is working quietly when a group of children start talking amongst themselves.

In a creative writing lesson, a child writes three short sentences and says he can't write any more.

Each incident was then presented to a sample of experienced primary school teachers and to a sample of student teachers who were individually asked (a) what more they would need to know in order to decide how to deal with the incident and (b) what their reaction would be. The two samples of teachers in fact responded quite differently. Generally, the experienced teachers reported a series of similar situations which they considered typical of their own classrooms, and commented upon how they would normally deal with them, whereas student teachers' reports were very much more restricted. For example, in responding to the above incident in which a group of children start talking, the experienced teachers generally identified situations such as the 'class clown' starting to 'play up', a child being unable to do his work and disturbing others, a distraction like a wasp flying around the room or the class making a noise when another teacher comes in, and these typical situations would often be associated with different reactions from the teacher. The student teachers on the other hand, distinguished far fewer situations, more often responding with overall 'blanket' reactions, as illustrated by one student who, replying to the same incident, said, 'I'd wait until the noise reached an intolerable level, then I'd tell them to shut up.'

In addition, the experienced teachers often reported taking account of the characteristics of the pupil(s) involved – the ability of the children, their attentiveness and whether a child was perceived as a 'clown' or a 'troublemaker', for example. This was in contrast to many of the student teachers, whose responses more often discriminated such features as the time of day or the importance of the lesson. For example, students frequently reported the need to maintain a greater control of classroom noise during 'formal' activities, such as mathematics or English, than during 'informal' activities like art and craft.

Comparing the experienced teachers' and student teachers' responses to these critical incidents reveals a marked difference in their working knowledge and demonstrates how experienced teachers have come to structure their knowledge of pupils, situations and classroom contexts together with their repertoire of teaching practices to enable classroom events to be readily identified and dealt with quickly and routinely.

In order to manage and instruct their classes effectively, beginning teachers have to accumulate considerable information about pupils, teaching materials, classroom and school and about the social context in which they will work. They must also consider the appropriateness of different teacher behaviours in different contexts, and become skilled in responding to their perceptions of events. Such knowledge and skill, however, is not easily gained and teachers often report that it is mostly learned by a process of trial and error, sometimes accompanied by considerable anxiety (Hanson and Herrington 1976, Evans 1976). During initial training, students may attempt to learn about teaching by observing experienced teachers at work, but this approach, as suggested earlier, is limited in the knowledge and skills it yields, since it is not always clear from observation alone what teachers are actually doing. The complexity of teachers' actions is often hidden from view and it is not always possible even for an experienced observer to appreciate fully what is happening. These difficulties are exemplified in the work of one postgraduate student and experienced secondary school teacher, who was investigating the special characteristics of teaching in small rural primary schools. In visiting a classroom and making notes of his observations he wrote that the teacher had left one group of pupils to *play with farmyard animals in the corner of the classroom*. On discovering this, the teacher concerned quickly corrected his description pointing out that far from playing, the pupils were engaged in sorting and matching, essential mathematical activities in the infant classroom! Such misinterpretations might not be expected of those who are more familiar with the infant school curriculum. Nevertheless, such instances reaffirm the difficulties of understanding classroom practice without access to the thoughts, intentions and decisions of teachers: difficulties which contribute to the plight of beginning teachers in their efforts to acquire a level of teaching competence. Ideally, more effective means are required for providing student teachers not only with the essential knowledge of pupils, materials and classroom context, but with a way of understanding teaching which enables them to appreciate how such knowledge is and could be used. Exploratory work that has been carried out in this field is discussed in later chapters.

THE MANAGEMENT OF EDUCATIONAL CHANGE

Studies of teacher decision-making also help to illuminate some of the difficulties involved in the complex processes of educational management and curriculum innovation. Although teachers are at the forefront of the educating process, many other personnel and corporate bodies are involved in the management and control of schools and the curriculum, and may therefore directly or indirectly influence teachers' classroom practice. Headteachers and promoted staff within the school and also school governors, educational administrators, curriculum designers, the DES, teacher training institutions and many others may all attempt to shape the nature of school and classroom life. Given the diversity of aims and interests that this includes and the complex inter-relationships of these individuals and agencies, it is hardly surprising that attempts to change the school curriculum are beset with difficulties. However, even when the relevant personnel, including teachers, are fairly well agreed about the promotion of certain innovations, attempts to implement them often meet with limited success.

The introduction of the Humanities Curriculum Project (Stenhouse 1970) in secondary schools provides one such example. The project consisted of a package of materials, including reading matter, posters and audio-visual aids on topics relating to social problems. The materials, together with a teacher's guide book, were intended to help teachers initiate class discussions on issues of interest to the pupils. In the early 1970s, the project was adopted by many secondary schools for use with non-examination classes, frequently replacing more formal geography, history or modern studies courses. Both the emphasis on discussion in contrast to reading and writing, and on topics of human interest in contrast to traditional subject matter were possibly appealing features of a package to be used with early school leavers. However, despite the attraction of the HCP, teachers encountered considerable difficulty in its implementation. In particular, their new role as an impartial discussion leader was one that proved almost impossible to achieve.

Various reasons were suggested for this difficulty. Some attributed blame to the teachers, suggesting that they were basically reluctant to relinquish their more traditional authoritarian teaching role. Others suggested that the pupils lacked interest in the topics, or that the curriculum developers had underestimated the managerial problems involved in teaching less able 15-year-olds, many of whom had no desire to be at school, the teacher having to adopt an authoritarian role in order to maintain control of such classes. A number of teachers were highly committed to the innovation and took part in in-service training courses to develop knowledge and skills relevant for implementing the project, yet still encountered great difficulty in putting these to work in their own classrooms (Aston 1980). Ruddock (1980), after interviewing a sample of pupils about their reactions to HCP lessons, speculates that pupils' views and reactions may have been responsible for some of these difficulties. She suggests that when pupils were introduced to the HCP they found themselves in an insecure and threatening situation: accustomed to a predominantly authoritarian, chalk-and-talk style of teaching, they were now expected (often for the first time) to discuss ideas and express their own opinions. They were uncertain how to respond and were suspicious of the innovation. Ruddock suggests that the pupils' consequent lack of interest and low level of co-operation in the project would inevitably be communicated to the teacher, perhaps leading the teacher to the conclusion that the HCP 'doesn't work'.

A similar fate to that of the HCP has befallen several other attempts to innovate the school curriculum, including efforts to change the emphasis of science teaching to the learning of scientific *processes* rather than the learning of scientific *knowledge* (see Olson 1980) and attempts to introduce 'progressive methods' or discovery learning into the junior school (see Galton, Simon and Croll 1980).

Because of the complex network of influences upon the curriculum, satisfactory explanations of why curriculum innovations frequently fail to be implemented as expected are often difficult to attain. However, research into the curriculum innovation process has frequently traced a major cause of failure to the difficulties experienced by teachers in adapting their style of teaching to satisfy the demands both of the new curriculum and to the existing school and classroom context (Doyle and Ponder 1977, Olson 1980). Consideration of the decision-making aspects of teaching and the context in which these occur can help to clarify the nature of some of these problems. As previously noted, experienced teachers have established lesson plans, and a repertoire of routines both for implementing these and for coping with everyday classroom situations. Innovations which require teachers to change their teaching procedures, or innovations which present new, unfamiliar classroom problems may necessitate teachers spending a considerable amount of time and effort in the sometimes difficult task of thinking out new plans and routines, a task in which they are generally given little assistance. Such is the nature of teaching that when faced with classroom situations requiring an immediate response the teacher may only be able to react with a familiar, well-practised routine, even though the innovation demands the invention of an alternative one. In addition, the context in which the teacher works may make certain new routines difficult or impossible to operate. Implementing discovery learning in some areas of the junior school curriculum, for example, presents enormous difficulties for a single teacher within the constraints of the normal classroom. In such cases, successful innovation depends not only upon new materials and ideas or assistance in acquiring new skills, but also upon a change in the organisational structure of classrooms and schools.

A fuller understanding of teaching processes in ordinary classrooms and of how these relate to different teaching contexts might help teachers and others engaged in shaping the curriculum to work more constructively and effectively towards the improvement of educational practices. Research on teacher decision-making can contribute to such an understanding and thereby aid the process of innovation.

The remaining chapters of this book examine how teachers' thoughts and decisions relate to particular areas of educational practice. Relevant research is discussed in relation to issues of interest and importance to teachers, starting with problems of classroom management and control in Chapter 2 and the issue of instructional effectiveness in Chapter 3. Decisions involved in planning and managing the curriculum are examined in Chapter 4, which leads into a discussion of the constraints upon teachers' decisions and classroom practice in Chapter 5. Chapter 6 reviews innovatory approaches to helping teachers to acquire the knowledge and skills for classroom competence, and considers further the role of research on teacher decision-making in helping teachers to understand and improve classroom practice.

RECOMMENDED READING

Hargreaves, D.H. (1979) 'A phenomenological approach to classroom

decision-making'. In Eggleston, J. (ed.) *Teacher Decision-Making in the Classroom*. London: Routledge & Kegan Paul.
    A brief and very readable account of the phenomenology (i.e. the experience) of teachers' everyday decision-making, based on Hargreaves' study of secondary school teachers' reactions to deviance in the classroom.
Jackson, P.W. (1968) *Life in Classrooms*. New York: Holt, Rinehart and Winston.
    A classic study in which Jackson describes the daily life of teachers and pupils in primary schools. Though a US study, it could equally well apply to schools in Britain. Pages 143–55 contain Jackson's account of the decision-making aspects of teaching.
Peterson, P.L. & Walberg, H.J. (eds) *Research on Teaching: Concepts, Findings and Implications*. California: McCutchan.
    This contains a series of papers reviewing research on teaching, with chapters on teacher effectiveness, teachers' decision-making and teachers' thinking.

EXERCISES

1. Recall some of the decisions that you have made today. How has your *process* of decision-making differed on these occasions? Were your decisions reflective, immediate or routine ones?
2. List some of the teaching routines that you regularly employ, or that you have observed other teachers employ. What do you think led to the development of each routine? In which contexts are the routines used? Are they, in your view, useful routines to acquire?
3. If you were planning a mathematics lesson for your class, what factors might influence/constrain your planning decisions? Would the same or different influences/constraints affect your planning of an art lesson?
4. List some of the unexpected interruptions/events that you have encountered in lessons, or have observed in other teachers' lessons. How did you or the teacher cope? Could these events have been anticipated? Suggest some alternative routines or strategies to cope with these events.

2

Classroom Management

INSTRUCTION AND MANAGEMENT

TEACHERS' professional practice is frequently described in terms of two major and apparently separate tasks. One is the task of *instruction*, involving the selection and sequencing of appropriate lesson content, the transmission of knowledge, skills and attitudes, and the provision of feedback to pupils about their learning progress. The other is the task of *classroom management*, involving the organisation of pupils and materials, the establishment of classroom procedures to facilitate the work of the class and dealing with disruptions and threats to classroom order. This division of teachers' tasks is somewhat artificial for these two areas of teacher activity are often closely intermeshed. In the case of experienced teachers, managerial strategies have sometimes become embedded in their everyday practice, inseparable from the whole business of teaching. A teacher may ask a question in such a way as to emphasise the importance of a specific piece of information, for example, but a particular child may be called upon to answer because he was gazing out of the window at the time. While introducing new material to a class or group, the teacher's tone of voice may be communicating the importance of pupil involvement. Similarly, the regular checking of pupils' work and quick responses to pupils' difficulties may serve both to manage as well as instruct the class.

However, for the beginning teacher, and even for some experienced ones, the task of management is not easy to master and integrate. Many of the concerns and anxieties of beginning teachers centre around difficulties of controlling pupil behaviour or organising the work of the class (Fuller and Bown 1975, Taylor 1975). These anxieties are not lessened by the fact that class management is an aspect of teaching that is highly valued in schools. Failure to control pupils' classroom behaviour or to manage the activities of a class can obviously have disastrous consequences for both pupils and teacher. When classroom order breaks down or becomes difficult to maintain, teaching becomes increasingly demanding and stressful and pupils learn little. In addition, teachers often fear that a breakdown of order and discipline in another teacher's class presents a threat to the control of their own. Consequently, it is perhaps not surprising that the amount of noise coming from a classroom and the degree of movement and disorder observed within it are cues which, in a school context, are frequently interpreted by colleagues and headteachers as a reflection not only of a teacher's classroom managerial competence, but of their total professional competence and the teacher's worth within the school.

Beginning teachers quickly learn the importance of classroom management. The most frequently mentioned comments from supervising tutors on student teaching practices concern control and management (see Hanson and Herrington 1976). The most common advice given by more experienced colleagues to beginning teachers on their entry into school is to establish authority at the beginning of the session, to be firm with the children, to beware of being perceived as 'soft', to achieve command of the class before attempting to teach anything, advice popularly abbreviated in the instruction, 'Don't smile until Christmas!' Unfortunately, the various means by which class control and effective management can be established are not so commonly or clearly articulated in the advice and folklore of teaching. Although teachers may well be effective managers themselves, they may find difficulty in analysing their practice to explain the real nature of their effectiveness. Yet, if beginning teachers are to acquire managerial competence other than through their own trial and error in the classroom, an understanding of the nature of classroom management and how it may be achieved is essential.

CLASSROOM MANAGEMENT AND TEACHER DECISION-MAKING

Effective classroom management can be viewed as essentially concerning the achievement and maintenance of pupils' involvement in teacher-prescribed or teacher-approved activities. When pupils are busily doing what the teacher requires of them, the teacher can be considered to be successfully managing the class. Effective management, defined in this way, involves teachers in decisions both in the pre-active phase of designing appropriate activities and in the interactive phase of implementing and maintaining them. Beginning teachers are often most concerned with the interactive decision-making demands of the task, in particular attempting to discover the best ways of responding to pupils' unco-operative or inattentive behaviour when it occurs. Research, however, suggests that teachers' approaches to dealing with disruption are not the most salient characteristic of effective classroom management, and beginning teachers' efforts to develop such strategies might well be misdirected. A series of studies led by Kounin (1970) for example, investigated primary school teachers' responses to disruptive incidents in their own classrooms. The researchers observed the teachers during normal classroom activities, and when disruptive incidents occurred, noted the nature of the incident and how the teacher dealt with it. They also noted certain features of each teacher's response such as its firmness, clarity, the extent to which it expressed anger and whether the response was successful at extinguishing the disruption. Kounin originally hypothesised that teachers judged to be effective classroom managers would respond differently to disruption from teachers judged to be less effective managers. However, no such difference was found. Surprisingly, both samples of teachers were observed to display a similar range of responses which were effective to a similar extent. Continued observation of these teachers led Kounin to discover that what distinguished the effective classroom managers was not their ability to cope with classroom disruptions once they arose, *but their ability to prevent disruption occurring in the first place*.

Kounin selected his samples of effective and ineffective managers on the basis of judgements made by observers on the amount of time pupils spent involved in classroom activities. Those teachers whose classes were observed to spend a high proportion of time engaged in classwork were selected as effective managers whereas those designated as less effective had classes which did not. A similar criterion for selecting samples of effective and ineffective managers was adopted by Anderson, Evertson and Emmer (1980) who in addition matched their two samples of teachers in terms of the age and general socioeconomic status of their classes. Through classroom observation, Anderson's study also attempted to identify the distinguishing features of effective managers in primary schools and largely confirmed the Kounin findings.

Both the Kounin and Anderson studies found that teachers achieved high levels of pupil involvement and avoided classroom disruption not through their handling of deviance and disruption, but through their careful *planning and design of activities*, through *the establishment of norms for classroom behaviour and work procedures* which enabled activities to be easily implemented and changed, and through a number of *classroom management skills* that ensured the efficient working of the class.

Moreover, supportive findings have emerged from studies of classroom management in secondary schools (Hargreaves et al. 1975, Partington and Hinchliffe 1979, Evertson and Emmer 1982, Wragg 1983). The essence of effective management, it would seem, lies in the types of *decisions made and strategies adopted in designing, implementing and maintaining activities.*

LESSON PLANNING FOR EFFECTIVE MANAGEMENT

Many of the classroom disruptions observed by Kounin appeared to arise from boredom and frustration. Pupils experiencing difficulty with their classwork or losing interest in it would frequently become restless, inattentive to the task at hand, and would start to disrupt the work of others in the class. Teachers who were effective managers minimised such disruptions by planning their lessons to provide activities which the children could successfully complete and by selecting activities which might arouse their interest.

As described in Chapter 1, planning activities involves making decisions about the content to be taught, which materials are to be used, who is to be involved in the activities and how the class is to be organised. In planning for effective management, these decisions depend upon teachers using their knowledge of pupils, lesson content, materials and forms of classroom organisation, and considering previous experiences of these, to design activities which will keep the class actively and constructively engaged. Clearly it would be an impossible task for teachers to accumulate and to plan activities appropriate to each. Many activities are therefore planned to cater for the estimated general interests and abilities of groups, or even of the whole class. Borko, Shavelson and Stern (1981), for example, found that primary school teachers, once they have grouped children for reading, plan instruction for the group rather than individual children. In the case of some pupils, however, those with low levels of concentration or those with particular learning difficulties for instance, a more detailed knowledge of the children's abilities is necessary in order to plan activities that will successfully maintain their attention. At times, such children can involve teachers in large amounts of planning. For example, a child with reading difficulties might be comfortably assigned to a group activity to which he could usefully contribute and in which others in the group will undertake the necessary reading, but if the class is to work individually in activities dependent on written materials, the teacher may have to plan to have time to spend with him, provide an alternative activity or prepare other materials such as a tape recording of the text.

The effective manager must also possess an extensive knowledge of the relevant subject matter, alternative ways of teaching it, and how it is best covered in a given context. Some subject matter may be easily made interesting and may therefore maintain pupil interest quite readily. Macabre topics such as the 'Black Death', 'skeletons', and 'surgery before the invention of anaesthetics' are well known to present few problems in maintaining some children's interest! Whereas the 'cummutative law of arithmetic' may require more inventive planning if it is to arouse interest in more than a small minority.

Teachers also possess useful knowledge about possible ways of organising their class, knowing which types of classroom organisation are most easily managed given the subject matter and pupils involved, and knowing how best to group the class when groups are required. Would a class lesson on a particular topic actively engage the whole class, or are the abilities and interests of the class sufficiently diverse that a number of different group activities would be necessary? Could a new principle be taught through a class game or would such an activity with these particular children simply lead to unnecessary noise, excitement and eventually chaos? Decisions such as these, made during lesson planning, are likely to influence the levels of productivity and attention to task within the classroom.

Planning also helps to attune and prepare teachers for various eventualities that could arise during the course of a lesson. As a result of planning, teachers may become aware that certain pupils may lose interest in the activity before it is completed, that some parts of the activity may provide difficulties for certain children, or that a few will complete the activity well before the others in the class and will therefore need further activities to proceed with.

Classroom management, however, cannot be the sole objective of teachers' lesson planning. Obviously teachers cannot plan activities simply to interest and occupy the children. Consideration must be given to what children ought to learn and teachers' planning decisions occur within a framework of constraints including a syllabus, a timetable and the availability of materials. These other aspects of planning are explored more fully in Chapter 4.

Nevertheless, planning aids classroom management by providing a framework for classroom activities, by preparing teachers for possible problems and difficulties that may arise, and perhaps also by increasing the resulting confidence with which teachers face their lessons, which in turn may make the classroom experiences of teachers less taxing. Effective management, however, cannot be attributed to planning alone. The planned activities must be implemented and maintained and these demand further decisions of teachers.

ESTABLISHING CLASSROOM NORMS

In some busy well-managed classrooms, particularly in primary schools, children engage in a variety of activities. They move freely about the room obtaining materials, consulting the teacher or changing activities apparently at will. The children appear purposeful and involved and although they may occasionally stop and talk to others they do not create a disturbing level of noise or engage in lengthy idle chatter. Even when the occasional crisis or difficulty arises in such classrooms, the teacher copes and the general flow of work within the class is not seriously disrupted.

Potentially, thirty or so pupils engaged in a variety of activities in one room with one supervising adult could result in chaos. But while some teachers find themselves unable to cope with such a situation, others establish and maintain this pattern of classroom organisation with apparent ease. To some extent, this may be attributed to the teacher's planning, ensuring that appropriate materials are available, and that the activities are reasonably well-matched to the pupils' abilities and interests, but their managerial success is also partly due to the establishment of norms or standards for classroom conduct, allowing activities to be easily and smoothly established and maintained. The children have come to know in which contexts it is appropriate to speak and in which it is not; they know for what purposes they are allowed to move around in the classroom and the purposes for which they must first seek permission; they know the behaviours that will be tolerated by the teacher and the sanctions that will be imposed should they exceed these limits.

The establishment of classroom norms is a process of negotiation, important in its consequences for both teacher and pupils. Where teachers fail to communicate or enforce acceptable procedures and behaviour, pupils will come to establish their own, possibly undesirable, less educationally productive ones. In both primary and secondary schools, effective classroom managers have been found to spend more time than their less effective colleagues communicating to pupils their expectations for classroom behaviour, explaining the procedures by which the work of the class is to be carried out, and the reasons for such procedures. Sometimes rules for classroom conduct and the procedures for particular activities are explicitly detailed. Wragg, for example, found that science teachers in particular spent much time at the beginning of the year, stressing the rules for conduct in the laboratory, and the procedures for obtaining, using and returning equipment. Similarly, Anderson found that effective managers in the primary school would often outline important classroom rules on the first day of term, and would even go to the extent of demonstrating how the children should carry their chairs when moving from their desks to the blackboard, for example, and explaining how they should line up at the door, when so instructed. The teachers would often also explain the need for these rules for the smooth operation of the classroom. Effective managers tended to stress the importance of their pupils' work and the need to establish efficient classroom procedures in which instruction and learning could take place. Though considerable time may be spent at the beginning of the year in demonstrating and explaining these procedures, once established they appear to reduce considerably the chaos of the classroom and the managerial demands upon teachers. Teachers' expectations for classroom conduct are also communicated and reinforced through the feedback given to pupils. By correcting examples of misbehaviour and praising appropriate behaviour, the teacher indicates expected behavioural norms. Praise and punishment are frequently used techniques for shaping pupil behaviour, and ensuring that required procedures and regulations are adhered to. However, although these techniques have become routine in many classrooms, they must be used discriminately in order to establish and maintain conformity. Actions which are intended to convey praise (e.g. comments such as 'Well done!', 'Good!' or a reward of special privileges) or disapproval (eye-contact, reproof, or more severely, the use of particular sanctions) are not always interpreted by pupils as expected, and may on some occasions have quite unintended effects. Deliberately praising a shy child in front of the class, for example, or praising a child who has close ties with a peer group holding strong anti-school and anti-teacher attitudes, may cause embarrassment, and even discourage the child from conforming. Brophy (1981) also points out that praise can fulfil a variety of functions, and in some cases is only a routine response, elicited on pupil demand – by bringing their work to show the teacher, or through expectant glances or tones of voice, some pupils may 'demand' routine approval. It is therefore not surprising that teacher and pupils can often form different views as to the significance of praise, and teachers' efforts to reward conformity can sometimes go unheeded (see Cooper and Good 1983).

Teachers may often use praise to reward effort or high achievement, aiming to encourage high standards of work in the future. Again, however, there is some evidence to suggest that emphasis upon rewards may lead to undesirable outcomes. Lepper (1983) reviews several studies which demonstrate that when activities are pursued by pupils for their extrinsic rewards, the intrinsic satisfaction of doing similar work in the future declines. Consequently, if teachers wish their pupils to experience satisfaction in carrying out school work, care has to be taken that praise or other rewards do not become an end in themselves.

Disapproval or punishment can be equally misinterpreted by pupils, leading also to undesired effects. If pupils feel that punishment is due to the teacher's dislike of them, for example, or to the teacher's blatant unreasonableness, it may simply lead to a deterioration in teacher-pupil relationships rather than direct pupils' attention to the correction of their own behaviour (see Worrall, Worrall and Meldrum 1983).

Clearly, praise and punishment must be handled warily in attempts to shape pupil behaviour and establish classroom norms. However, based on present research evidence, a number of general guidelines can be offered which might help teachers develop appropriate strategies. *First*, it would seem important that pupils understand what is being praised or punished and why. Teachers' actions might therefore be more effective if they occur soon after the behaviour concerned, and if teachers explicitly relate their praise or punishment to specific behaviours. *Second*, praise or punishment is likely to be more effective if it is viewed by the pupils as justified. Praise should therefore be sincere and warranted. If pupils perceive praise as a routine teacher's comment or merely a reflection of the teacher's mood, it might lose any rewarding effect. Similarly, punishment should be perceived as constructive and deserved. When pupils 'break the rules' the teacher's reprimand might be usefully accompanied by a reiteration of the reasons for having the rules, stressing their importance for the work of the class and by some encouragement to behave appropriately in future. Particular sanctions could also be chosen to emphasise the teacher's rationale (e.g. staying in to complete work at break to make up for the time lost through unnecessary talking). *Third*, in praising or punishing, teachers must take full account of the pupils and the school and classroom context. Punishment which is out of line with school practice, for example, or praise which is unwelcome, may have quite unintended effects. Teachers must become aware of how their actions in the classroom are likely to be interpreted.

Effective managers have also been found to check periodically that their pupils have understood and remembered the classroom procedures and regulations that are established early in the term. For example, in the following transcript, an excerpt from the afternoon activities of a class of 7–8 year olds, the teacher is ensuring that the pupils have remembered the preliminary procedures for painting, before directing one group of pupils to the painting corner:

T: All the elephants [the name of one of the groups in the class] can do some painting in the corner. But before you go, what's the first thing you will do when you are over there?
P: Get some newspaper out of the cupboard.
T: Right, and what's the second thing you'll do?
P: Cover the table.
T: Yes, cover the table all over with newspaper so it doesn't get messy. And then what will you do? Fiona.
P: Get the paints and some water.
T: Fine, but remember not to put too much water in the jars because it will just spill over, won't it?

In this example, the teacher is both checking that the pupils know the required procedure for starting a painting activity and reminding them of the reasons for this procedure.

As children's experience of schooling grows and they encounter a variety of teachers, they develop a general impression of what is expected of them in a classroom context. However, they also discover that teachers are somewhat idiosyncratic, holding different levels of tolerance for pupils' misbehaviour in different classroom activities as the following interview with a secondary school pupil indicates.

I: What sort of rules do you have in classrooms?
P: No talking, no moving about, no chewing and just get on with your work.
I: When you say no talking, is that all of the time?
P: Yes, well, sometimes you can talk in classes, then in other classes you can do what you want. In Art we can work if we want and if we don't want to we don't. With Mr — we have to work all the time and if he sees anything wrong then he does one of his karate chops on you. Sometimes he lets you talk. He lets it go so far and then he tells you to shut up.
I: When are the times that you can't talk?
P: Well, if we're having a test or we're reading. Sometimes we can talk amongst ourselves and to the teacher about things, but when we are doing work we are not allowed to talk.

I: You said that you're not allowed to move. Is that all the time?
P: Well, in some lessons. In Miss —'s you're allowed to move about and in
     Science, but not in English and Maths. If you move about in Mr —'s, he
     slaps you across the back. You can only talk when he goes out of the
     room; we can talk quietly then. You can only move·if you're going to
     see him. In Mr —'s if you were chatting to your mates and getting on
     with your work it's all right.
I: What sort of talking would he not allow?
P: Swearing and shouting.
I: Are there times in lessons when you can talk?
P: Yes, when the teacher goes out of the room or when she says, 'What
     were you doing at the weekend?' Or when we've come back from
     holidays.... And when we're doing projects or something like that
     we can talk, or we're doing a display on the wall. We go and get
     ideas from other people.
I: What about those times when you're definitely not allowed to talk?
P: When we're having a test or something or when we're writing off the
     board.

Excerpt from an interview between interviewer (I) and pupil (P),
from Hargreaves, Hester and Mellor (1975) (pp. 38–39).

Pupils can clearly be quite perceptive in distinguishing the expectations of different teachers and the contexts for which these expectations
hold. They obviously also link such expectations to teachers' idiosyncra-
cies in their choice of sanctions!

Given the different expectations of teachers and the different
inducements and sanctions they employ in negotiating norms, it is not
surprising that the first few contacts between a class and a new teacher,
particularly when older children are concerned, are generally characterised by the pupils attempting to assess and *try out* the teacher. Once the
teacher has asserted the rules of the game and appears consistent and
capable in enforcing them, classroom life may settle down. However, in
a few contexts, particularly with some adolescent pupils rebellious
against rules and regulations, this phase can develop into a power
struggle in which both teacher and pupils battle for supremacy. On the
pupils' part, battle may take the form of defiant non-co-operation.
Teachers, however, have often developed rather subtle means of
asserting their authority. In a case study of one teacher, Smith and
Geoffrey (1968) describe how Geoffrey, the teacher, started off the year
'grooving' the children. By giving the pupils relatively uncontentious
duties to perform, such as handing out books or sharpening the pencils,

Geoffrey attempted to break the children in gently to the notion that the teacher is the one in charge who gives orders, the pupils carry them out. Similar cues are sometimes provided by teachers when they tell the pupils at the beginning of the year where in the classroom they are going to sit, or by insisting upon conformity to relatively minor rules like 'coats in the cloakroom and bags under the desks'. Hanson and Herrington (1976) describe one teacher who adopted a rather more eccentric strategy. When feeling that the pupils were losing sight of his authority, he would insist at the end of the school day when the pupils had put the chairs on the table that they take the chairs down again and put them up properly, sometimes repeating the process two or three times. The pupils were not carrying out his instructions improperly on the first occasion, but this was viewed by the teacher as an opportunity to reaffirm who was boss. Such strategies, however, in order to serve their function require a confident appearance, and depend upon the teacher's bluff not being called. For some pupils and some teachers, they may be used dangerously, for to be drawn into petty disputes about who sits where or how the chairs are put on the tables would be a far from promising start to the beginning of term.

It is in the first few weeks of contact between teacher and pupils that much of the activity involving the negotiation of classroom norms occurs. Once negotiated, the norms greatly influence the running of the class for the rest of the year and, as most beginning teachers painfully discover, if undesirable norms for behaviour are allowed to become established early in the year they are extremely difficult to renegotiate at a later time. The norms have become accepted and children are resentful of attempts to change them. Establishing classroom norms often presents difficulties for beginning teachers. This is probably not because the strategies themselves are difficult to employ, but because student teachers rarely see experienced teachers using them and might not have acquired the appropriate knowledge.

The first few weeks of term when classroom norms are negotiated are rarely observed on student teaching practices. Even when they are, the behaviour of experienced teachers may not always provide a useful guide. When experienced teachers have taught in the same school for several years, their expectations for classroom conduct may have become communicated down through successive year-groups of pupils. Teachers may in fact be so well stereotyped by the pupils as a result of these expectations, that their confident appearance and authoritative tone of voice may be sufficient to remind pupils of them. Consequently, establishing behaviour and procedural norms in the classroom may demand far less attention from the experienced teacher than it deserves from the novice.

MANAGING PUPILS AND ACTIVITIES

Effective managers in both primary and secondary schools have repeatedly been found to teach lessons which are more fluent, contain fewer interruptions and involve smoother transitions between activities than those of less effective managers (Kounin 1970, Partington and Hinchliffe 1979, Anderson, Evertson and Emmer 1981). This can again be partly attributed to the thoughtful planning of the teachers and to the successful establishment of norms for classroom behaviour and work procedures, ensuring that the work of the class is completed in a well-organised fashion. However, even in lessons which are well matched to pupils' abilities and interests, and in classrooms where the pupils acknowledge the expectations for classroom conduct, managerial problems still arise. Interruptions and unforeseen difficulties occur and in these situations effective managers have been found to cope more successfully. The effective manager closely monitors classroom activities and exhibits a keen awareness of what is going on. This appears to facilitate classroom management in two quite separate ways. First, the pupils quickly realise that the teacher is well attuned to what they are doing, and once it is appreciated that the teacher has 'eyes in the back of her head' they are less likely to break classroom rules owing to the high risk of being caught out. Second, when potential disruption is identified early, it can be dealt with before it escalates into something more serious, therefore creating less distraction. Effective managers, in fact, have been found to have several routines for checking minor disruptions without interrupting the flow of the lesson at all – silencing a talkative group in the corner, for example, with a reproachful glance and a snapping of fingers, while continuing to listen to another child read – or for adjusting the pace or nature of the work in response to pupils' difficulties.

Monitoring the involvement of individual pupils in the class would clearly be difficult due to the size of most classes, the possible variety of activities going on and the other classroom demands upon teachers' time. Consequently, teachers have to be highly selective in their attention to classroom behaviours. The performance of certain pupils may be more closely monitored than that of others, for example, because the teacher suspects that they may have difficulty with the task or that their attention may easily wander. In observing some classes, it is often noticeable that although the pupils in general are allowed considerable freedom of movement and the teacher appears almost not to notice where individual pupils are going, there are one or two children who as soon as they stand up attract the teacher's attention and alert her to potential disruption. In other cases, the teacher may attend to group cues, such as the noise level and work rate within groups, as a more manageable way of gaining the information needed (Doyle 1979, Prawat 1980). Noise coming from a group may act as a signal that all is not well, and teachers may either rely upon their knowledge of the pupils involved to make an instant diagnosis of the problem (*It's John being a nuisance again*, or *This group is talking because they have finished*) or investigate the nature of the problem, before dealing with it.

Once teachers have established norms for classroom behaviour and procedures for classroom activities, and once the teacher has become familiar with the class and the personalities of the pupils within it, deviations from normal behaviour can be more easily identified. Teachers readily notice when pupils are engaging in less enthusiastic hand-raising than usual, or when the pupils look restless, tired or mischievous. Experienced teachers have learned to read the faces of their pupils, noticing, for example, the impish expressions of pupils attempting to hide something from the teacher, or the class's avoidance of eye contact that signifies loss of interest.

Acquiring this information from moment to moment in the classroom is, however, only part of the task of managing pupils and activities. In addition to selecting and interpreting cues, the teacher must also be able to respond to them quickly and appropriately in order to prevent disruptions escalating or to redirect the children's distracted attention to class work. Experienced teachers have developed repertoires of routines for coping with these everyday situations, enabling rapid responses. For example, as teachers talk to the whole class, they may automatically walk towards a part of the room where children appear inattentive in order to signal to the pupils that they are expected to listen. On other occasions, they may have a set of remedial strategies that are automatically employed when pupils experience difficulty with a new concept or procedure. Many teachers ensure that they learn the names of their pupils early in the term so that if pupils misbehave or fail to attend, reprimands or reminders can be easily directed towards the appropriate target, as opposed to relying on more general commands issued to the class or group.

Managerial routines may often be intertwined in the process of instruction and this is well exemplified in lessons in which teachers engage in much questioning of the class or group. An investigation, involving the collection of stimulated recall commentaries of primary school teachers, revealed a number of reasons for teachers' questioning and identified a common sequence (Calderhead 1979). Teachers would typically start a class lesson by asking questions of enthusiastic, able pupils – those who were first with their hand up, for example, who were likely to provide correct answers quickly. This enabled the teachers to establish rapport, to set the pace of the interaction and also to demonstrate to the less able in the class what the teacher expected them to do. Once these functions were fulfilled, teachers would then direct questions to the less able children to check that they had understood and were following the lesson – the teacher could then judge how to pace the lesson appropriately, minimising the chances of the able becoming bored and the less able being left behind. The teachers were also conscious of having to distribute their questions fairly evenly around the class, matching the difficulty of questions to the ability of pupils, and keeping the children on their toes by addressing questions to pupils in different parts of the room. Questions were also directed towards pupils who appeared inattentive in order to redirect their attention. If the pace of the lesson slowed down (for example when a number of children in succession had taken a long time to answer the teacher's questions) the teacher would then return to the able, eager pupils to accelerate the flow of the lesson and regain lost interest, at the same time making a mental note that some pupils in the class might be either having difficulty or losing interest in the topic, and require more individual attention later. During these periods of interaction with the whole class, the teachers closely monitored the process, sifting out cues indicating levels of pupil understanding and involvement, and using this information, together with their existing knowledge of the pupils and of the activities they had planned, to guide their actions and ensure the efficient management of the class. For the experienced teacher and effective classroom manager such procedures are probably a frequent but largely automatic part of their everyday teaching.

OTHER DETERMINANTS OF EFFECTIVE MANAGEMENT

The decisions made by teachers in planning lessons to satisfy the interests and abilities of pupils, in establishing behavioural norms and efficient working procedures, and in the early detection and remediation of pupil difficulties and distractions, have all been found in research to relate to the levels of pupil involvement in activities and the extent of classroom disruption. However, the style of management suggested by this research to be effective may not be the only successful one. Researchers on classroom management have typically searched for strategies common to a majority of effective managers. In reality, teachers may adopt these to different extents or may even employ alternative strategies not yet identified in research. The observation of teachers in any large school would probably reveal a wide range of management styles. For example, some teachers appear to achieve effective management largely through enforcing conformity to an explicitly communicated system of classroom rules, and a set of clear sanctions for rule-breaking. Others seem to rely more heavily upon keeping children involved in work that is interesting and well-matched to their abilities. Occasionally, however, teachers can be found who have quite unusual management styles. For example, the managerial effectiveness of some teachers might be mostly attributable to the exceptionally good relationship and mutual understanding the teachers have established with their children which seems to result in a co-operative working environment. Such teachers are probably few in number, but it is as well to remember that the management style described by research may not be the only one that 'works'. Teachers with different beliefs and values concerning how classrooms ought to be organised and finding themselves in different contexts may adopt variants of the style or indeed different styles altogether.

Effective classroom management cannot therefore be entirely reduced to competence in the three areas discussed so far. In fact, a number of other factors, some of which are beyond teachers' control, seem likely to determine how effectively teachers might manage their classes.

The relationship between teachers' personality and classroom management, for example, has not been a fruitful area for educational research, yet teachers themselves often associate certain aspects of personality such as self-confidence, dominance and assertiveness with managerial effectiveness. Certainly, one could reasonably expect that the way in which a teacher is perceived by pupils may either facilitate or hinder the teacher's success in establishing behavioural norms and in obtaining the co-operation of the class. And research on pupils' perceptions of teachers (see Cohen and Manion 1981) does in fact suggest that both primary and secondary school children expect their teachers to be authority figures, preferring teachers who are strict, but also fair and sympathetic. Consequently, the teacher who is self-confident and assertive, but who can also relate to the pupils, may more easily match the children's expectations, and may therefore find it less troublesome to obtain their co-operation.

Partington and Hinchliffe (1979), after observing a sample of secondary school teachers, suggest that the effects of teachers' personalities upon management may depend upon the context. For example, they noted that extrovert teachers were more able to maintain interest and attention in lessons in which the teacher was required to perform before the class. However, when children were engaged in individual or group work, the teacher's extrovert personality would often result in distractions and such teachers would often find it difficult to adopt an unobtrusive teaching role.

While some beginning teachers may find it relatively easy to slip into the expected teacher role and thus derive the benefits from it, others, particularly in their very first classroom experiences, may find the maintenance of a self-confident, assertive image more strenuous.

Young teachers with classes of adolescents sometimes also find that age and even the status of being a student teacher or a new teacher has additional implications for how they are perceived by pupils. Whereas teachers similarly aged to the pupils' parents may be quite readily viewed as authority figures, a teacher only a few years older than the pupils themselves is less willingly given the same recognition. Similarly, in some schools, once pupils know that a teacher is a student or once they catch sight of the fresh-faced, enthusiastic expression that has come to signify fair game, teacher-baiting may well begin. To cope with such difficulties the teacher's salvation may lie in being accepted by the pupils as a 'proper teacher', a process which often seems to be enhanced if the student identifies with the school staff and is seen by pupils to be supported and respected by other staff. Unfortunately, given the students' uncertain status, students are sometimes tempted to identify with the pupils, projecting themselves as reasonable, tolerant and 'one of the lads', actions which often result in increased resentment from the class who do not wish to establish, or are not used to establishing, that type of relationship with adults.

Although little can be done to change teachers' personality or age, students who have difficulty in presenting themselves convincingly in the classroom have been found to benefit from viewing video-tapes of their lessons and discussing their performance with a sympathetic tutor. Video recordings enable students to scrutinise their sometimes unconscious mannerisms and direct their attention to the cues that pupils may interpret as hesitancy, uncertainty or incompetence. Students' observations of one another on classroom practices and discussions of their performances afterwards have also been found in some teacher training courses to fulfil a similar function.

The effectiveness of teachers' managerial strategies may also depend upon certain features of the school and its organisation. Effective classroom managers in a small rural school who move to an inner city comprehensive may have to adjust their expectations for pupil behaviour, tune in to a different set of cues in the classroom and develop alternative strategies for lesson planning and for dealing with classroom disruption in order to manage classes with comparable success. One teacher who made this transition recounted to the author the changes that had occurred in his teaching, particularly in his use of language, after his first few days at a large comprehensive. Instructions which had once been given as polite reminders – 'Would you mind closing the door, please?' – were found to be ignored by pupils or were met with puzzled expressions. In consequence, these were quickly and intuitively substituted with louder requests of a more imperative form – 'Boy, Door!'

Class size, the spread of ability within a class, and the general socioeconomic status of the pupils in the school have all been found to influence teachers' managerial behaviour. Large classes or a wide spread of ability often force teachers into engaging in more small group or individualised instruction (Bredo 1980, Evertson and Hickman 1981). Consequently, the teacher can become involved in planning a greater number of activities and managing a more complex environment. In such situations, teachers frequently reduce their work by relying on worksheets and self-instructional materials. Little is known about the resulting effects on the quality of pupils' learning experiences although investigation in this area would be of obvious value not only to teachers but in informing policy decisions concerning vertical grouping in primary schools, and mixed ability teaching in secondary schools. In the case of teachers with classes of predominantly working-class pupils it has sometimes been reported that they are more custodial in their classroom management than those of middle-class children (e.g. Bredo 1980).

The effectiveness of teachers' managerial efforts may also be determined by the curriculum. Hargreaves (1982) argues that the curriculum of the modern comprehensive school has largely failed to take up the challenge of providing a useful education for all children. He suggests that, under the pressure of the examination system and the value placed upon paper qualifications in society, the curriculum of the typical comprehensive has become a watered-down version of that of the old grammar school. The curriculum is geared towards examination success in O levels and A levels which gain entry to higher education. The nature of the curriculum is largely academic and is perceived as irrelevant by all but the few who make the transition to college or university. Furthermore, because of the academic nature of the curriculum and the few who benefit from it, school for the majority of children presents experiences of failure. Presented with a curriculum which seems irrelevant and in which they cannot succeed, Hargreaves suggests that children become alienated from the school system. They resent its values and opt out.

Clearly, in such situations teachers may find themselves with classes where the children have mostly 'switched off' from learning and do not see any value in what school has to offer. The curriculum, over which the teacher herself may have very limited influence, may be largely responsible for the managerial problems with which she has to cope.

It has also been suggested that the economic climate of the day may influence the nature and extent of the managerial problems that teachers face in the classroom. Pupils' loss of interest in school work and the recent rise in levels of violence in schools have been attributed to the drastic fall in employment prospects for school leavers (see Tattum 1982). Whereas in the past some children could be motivated to work with the promise of leaving with qualifications or a good report and thereby getting a job, the motivation dwindles when even the well-qualified find themselves on the dole.

Teachers, particularly those in inner-cities or in socially deprived areas where schools may appear less relevant to their pupils, can therefore encounter managerial problems which are caused by factors beyond the school and over which teachers have no control. In such situations, teachers may attempt to cope or merely to survive (see Chapter 5).

COPING WITH DIFFICULT PUPILS

For many teachers, classroom management consists largely of the routine establishment and maintenance of classroom activities. Acts of indiscipline which disrupt these activities are mostly breaches of relatively minor classroom rules. Unnecessary or excessive talking is by far the most common managerial problem faced by both primary and secondary school teachers, and the vast majority of teachers' reprimands are designed to curb noise (Jackson 1968, Hargreaves et al. 1975). However, not all children engage in normal behaviour in the classroom or respond to normal methods of classroom management. On a few occasions, and again more frequently for teachers in inner-city schools or schools in socially deprived areas, serious acts of disruption and instances of vandalism and personal violence may be confronted.

In most schools, pupils committing serious moral and legal infringements would be referred to a senior member of staff, the headteacher, deputy head, or in the case of a secondary school, the head of department or head of year group. In these cases, identifying the causes of the pupil's misbehaviour may determine the most appropriate action to be taken.

Basically 'normal' children who have committed a serious offence – a mischievous prank that went too far, for example – may be dealt with by ensuring that they appreciate the foolishness of their behaviour and make amends in some way. In other cases, the help of parents may be sought to control pupils' future behaviour in school, or the school may have a policy of corporal punishment. Where the child's behaviour is thought to be due to difficulties with learning, social adjustment or problems encountered at home, an educational psychologist, school counsellor, or social worker may be called in to assist. When a child's disruptive behaviour has clinical or social origins there is often no simple solution, however, and the problem behaviour may not be easily remedied or even contained in the short term.

Consequently, classroom teachers can still find themselves having to cope with difficult and disruptive pupils in the classroom and this can present a number of anxiety-provoking dilemmas. For example, a pupil who is persistently disruptive may delight in distracting the attention of other pupils in the class. The pupil's behaviour may not itself be sufficiently deviant to be regarded in the school as a matter for referral to a higher authority. To refer the child may be perceived by the pupils as a sign of weakness, an inability to cope, and might therefore lead to a reduced level of respect for the teacher and attract still further disruption. Not referring the child necessitates the teacher alone finding a way of coping.

Teachers may also find themselves dealing with pupils with emotional or clinical problems, whose behaviour is not sufficiently disruptive to warrant exclusion from the school or whose attendance at a normal school, rather than a special school, is thought to be desirable. When pupils respond to such problems by being introverted or withdrawn, teachers have been found to cope with them relatively easily in a classroom situation, often responding sympathetically and attempting to compensate for their disadvantage (Jackson 1968, Mackay and Marland 1978, Kedar-Voivodas and Tannenbaum 1979). However, pupils who respond to such difficulties in a disruptive manner present another dilemma for the teacher. Knowing the home life or clinical history of a pupil may lead a teacher to tolerate a certain amount of their disruptive behaviour, but the teacher also has a responsibility to the others in the class. In deciding whether and how to respond to a disruptive child, a teacher may have to consider the pupil's influence upon the work of the class and whether permitting misbehaviour from one exceptional child may be perceived as unfair by the other pupils or whether it may encourage others to follow the example and misbehave as well.

In coping with difficult pupils who do not conform to classroom rules, teachers frequently negotiate a contract. Sometimes the contract is explicit. By identifying what the pupil enjoys doing, the teacher may be able to trade certain privileges for good behaviour. For example, if a pupil likes to play football with the school team or if they want to take part in an extra-curricular activity organised by the school, participation in this can be made dependent upon the pupil's good behaviour in the classroom. Negotiating with disruptive pupils, however, can be quite a difficult task, as indicated in an interesting study by McCuller and Moseby (1983). They investigated disruptive and non-disruptive secondary school pupils' responses to a series of video-taped classroom situations concerning conflict between teachers and pupils. Non-disruptive pupils tended to report the teacher being right and were perceptive in identifying the feelings and emotions of the teacher and pupil involved in the incidents. Disruptive pupils, however, often perceived the teacher to be at fault and were less socially perceptive: they failed to notice teachers' sarcasm, for example, or the attitudes of those involved. When disruptive pupils believe their disruption to be justified and teachers to be at fault, and when they fail to tune in to some of the cues teachers communicate about their attitudes to disruptive events, negotiation is certain to be a demanding task.

In many cases, therefore, it is not surprising that attempts to negotiate a contract do not lead to very constructive ends. When teachers' attempts to control a child's disruption have repeatedly failed, they are sometimes found to have negotiated an unspoken contract in which the teacher agrees virtually to ignore the child, allowing him or her to produce a minimal amount of work in the classroom, as long as they refrain from disrupting the rest of the class (Smith and Geoffrey 1969, Nash 1973, Hargreaves et al. 1975). The teacher trades work for peace in the classroom. Although such a solution may seem unsatisfactory and may be perceived by some as an abdication of responsibility, the teacher may be responding as best as is possible given the classroom situation. Indeed, satisfactory solutions to the problems presented by difficult pupils again may often be beyond the control of individual teachers.

With the numbers of disruptive pupils increasing, particularly in secondary schools and in inner-city areas, many schools have sought organisational solutions to the problems they present. Some secondary schools have established disruptive pupil units, popularly referred to as 'sin bins', rooms or buildings in which pupils who do not easily settle into a classroom environment can be educated separately, often in small groups and focusing on a practical rather than academic curriculum. The introduction of school counsellors, the improvement of remedial facilities and the adaptation of the curriculum to cater for a wider range of interests, particularly those of the less academically inclined, are other common organisational responses to the problem of educating potentially difficult pupils.

Such responses, however, have given rise to a number of debates concerning both issues of moral principle and questions concerning the efficacy of the organisational change. Whether some pupils should be provided with a radically different curriculum from others, thus ultimately qualifying them for a different range of occupational choices, raises questions concerning equality of opportunity and the fundamental purposes of education. A study of US high schools by Duke and Meckel (1979) also questions whether attempts by US schools to cope with indiscipline by the appointment of special teachers, counsellors and administrators with responsibility for school discipline might actually have led to an *increase* rather than decrease in indiscipline within schools. Duke and Meckel argue that once personnel are appointed to hold special responsibility for school discipline, ordinary classroom teachers tend to relinquish their own responsibilities in this area and come to view the maintenance of appropriate pupil behaviour as someone else's job! All pupils therefore receive fewer cues about the expectations for their classroom behaviour. In addition, the new personnel involved with school discipline seek out different roles and relate to the children in different ways. Counsellors, for example, may view their role as a supportive one, helping disadvantaged children; special teachers may view theirs as one of diagnosing the knowledge and skills of pupils and providing them with appropriate educational tasks; and administrators may view theirs as one of involving the appropriate personnel in working with disruptive pupils. As a result of these different experts relating to the pupils in different ways, different impressions are communicated regarding the nature and acceptability of their behaviour, confusing the pupils' notions of appropriate conduct and leading to greater difficulties in the establishment of desirable behaviour norms within the school.

Organisational and curricular change clearly has an important part to play if schools are to cope more adequately with pupils who are disruptive and possibly alienated from the life of the school. If teachers are to succeed in educating all their pupils, attention must be given to the constraints that prevent them from doing so. It is also clear, however, that change must be based upon an understanding of the teacher's work within an institutional and curricular context so that changes in the context do not in fact worsen the problem they were intended to alleviate. At present, our understanding of this context and its effect upon classroom practice is limited and in need of considerable expansion.

IMPLICATIONS FOR BEGINNING TEACHERS

It was stated at the start of this chapter that beginning teachers commonly view effective classroom management as the employment of a few routine reactions in response to classroom deviance, and that they therefore often seek solutions to their managerial difficulties in terms of developing appropriate reactions to classroom incidents. However, such an approach to classroom management may not help to solve certain managerial problems and may even contribute to them. For example, it is not uncommon to find beginning teachers or indeed, some more experienced ones, repeatedly shouting 'Be quiet!' to the continual eruptions of classroom talking when the noise itself is a symptom of lack of interest or task difficulty, and demands quite a different response. Similarly, when beginning teachers encounter unanticipated difficulties – suddenly discovering that pupils do not possess the knowledge that had been taken for granted, or misjudging the reactions of pupils to a lesson – it disrupts the flow of activities and may lead to loss of interest and deviance, yet this could have been avoided had the problems been identified at an earlier stage. In addition, beginning teachers, particularly in their first few experiences in the classroom, are sometimes preoccupied with implementing their planned lesson to the extent that monitoring of pupils and activities is minimal, resulting in inattention and disruption. Such teaching difficulties are not peculiar to beginning teachers alone, but are quite common at the start of a teaching career. In contrast, the findings of research indicate that teachers' managerial decision-making involves considerably more than reacting to deviance, and that these common difficulties could be largely avoided if beginning teachers' efforts to master classroom management were channelled in a number of other directions.

First of all, effective management would seem to depend on effective lesson planning in which teachers use their knowledge of pupils, subject matter and classroom organisation to design activities which are likely to interest the pupils, allow them to succeed and which can be easily managed in the classroom with minimal opportunity for disruption.

Beginning teachers clearly need to consider *the knowledge, skills and interests of the pupils they will teach, the nature of the subject matter involved and how it is best incorporated into classroom activities*. They need to have a clear idea in mind of how their lessons will progress, anticipate what may go wrong, and be prepared to cope with these eventualities.

Second, beginning teachers will have to develop *clear notions of the standards of behaviour* they expect from pupils and communicate these consistently, especially in the first few contacts with the class, in order to establish norms for classroom conduct. Efficient work procedures, which stress the importance of learning and which can become routine for the pupils, can also be developed to increase pupils' attention to classwork. Supervising teachers may have to be consulted or observed to become familiar with the norms and work procedures and the means of establishing these, so that procedures are used which pupils will understand and to which they are likely to respond.

Anticipating organisational and learning difficulties in the classroom is a third area of managerial competence to be developed by beginning teachers. Learning to monitor classroom activities, even when teachers themselves are in interaction, requires an ability to discriminate cues which signal pupil involvement, and a knowledge of which pupils and in which activities more intensive monitoring may be required. With experience, beginning teachers will probably come to read their pupils, using such cues as eye contact, hand raising, facial expressions and group noise in order to identify potential disruptions. As well as the early identification of inattention and disturbance, beginning teachers must develop a series of strategies appropriate for dealing with these situations, strategies which themselves create minimal disturbance, and which with practice, will become routine. Again, observation of teachers and discussion with teachers and tutors would seem important in the development of such skills.

In addition to these three areas of managerial competence identified by research, beginning teachers may also find it useful to give some thought to *how they are to present themselves as teachers* in the classroom and to the *institutional context* in which they work. It seems likely that pupils will be more co-operative and accept the norms imposed by teachers if they perceive them as fair-minded and pleasantly strict. It should also be remembered that teachers function within an institution that can help or hinder their attempts to manage the class. It would obviously be useful for beginning teachers to consider school policies and practices regarding classroom management, and how these relate to their own practices – what standards of behaviour are expected in the school? What sanctions are meted out, by whom, and on what occasions are they appropriate? What assistance is available within the school should the teacher encounter particularly troublesome pupils?

The beginning teacher, in order to become an effective manager, must clearly amass a vast amount of knowledge and develop numerous classroom skills. Some of this knowledge and skill can be developed from lectures and personal discussions with tutors, from observing and talking to teachers in schools, and from practice within classrooms. However, students learning to teach need to know what kinds of things to notice about teachers and pupils, how they should be cued in to understanding teaching and reflecting upon their own classroom practice. In this context, research and development work on teaching and teacher education has an important role to play. Research on classroom management, for example, provides a fuller understanding of the processes of management and can guide students to more appropriate solutions to the managerial problems they face. In addition, it can describe some of teachers' working knowledge and how this is used to guide teachers' classroom practice. In so doing, research cannot provide a series of ready recipes to be employed mindlessly upon immediate entry to the classroom since teachers find themselves in a unique context and will express different preferences in their selection of teaching strategies. However, by making teachers' working knowledge explicit, research exemplifies the type of knowledge that is used and provides a sample from which beginning teachers can select, modify and experiment in the process of developing their own managerial practices. Research on classroom management has also led to the development of a number of workbooks and training courses for beginning teachers (see Wragg 1981, Evertson, et al. 1981, Borg and Ascione 1982) in which training exercises are presented with the aim of helping teachers notice the relevant skills in management and develop them in their own practice. The nature of these training materials and their effects upon classroom management processes are discussed in Chapter 6.

RECOMMENDED READING

Docking J.W. (1980) *Control and Discipline in Schools: perspectives and approaches*. London: Harper & Row.

A comprehensive review of issues concerning classroom management and the control of children's behaviour in school. Outlines different explanations for deviant behaviour and examines the supporting evidence and implicit values in alternative control strategies.

Hargreaves, D.H., Hester, S.K. & Mellor, F.J. (1975) *Deviance in Classrooms*. London: Routledge & Kegan Paul.

A study of how secondary school teachers come to identify and react to deviance in their classrooms.

King, R. (1978) *All Things Bright and Beautiful?* Chichester: John Wiley.

A study of three infant schools of widely different social composition. Chapter 6 considers infant teachers' control strategies.

Saunders, M. (1979) *Class Control and Behaviour Problems*. London: McGraw-Hill.

Examines the causes and possible treatments of disruptive and maladjusted children in a school context, and describes the roles of supportive agencies, such as the schools psychology service, and social services.

Tattum, D. (1982) *Disruptive Pupils in Schools and Units*. Chichester: John Wiley.
Describes recent provisions for disruptive pupils, both in and out of school. Examines pupils' own accounts of their disruptive behaviour, and in the light of these, considers the effects of alternative provisions on pupils.

EXERCISES

1. List some of the norms for classroom conduct that you would wish to establish with your class at the beginning of the year (e.g. regarding talking, working procedures and classroom behaviour). How would you establish them? What sanctions might you use for children who transgress these norms, and what would determine your choice of sanction? Discuss your answers with your tutor or an experienced teacher.

2. Observe a teacher engaging in a 'recitation' style of classroom interaction (ie. rapid-fire questioning). Try to identify, from the context in which they occur:

    (a) why the questions take the form they do;
    (b) why the questions are asked of particular pupils.

    Check out your interpretations with the teacher afterwards (a tape recorder would be useful here if the teacher does not object). How do your interpretations and the teacher's compare? What cues does the teacher take note of during the session? What questioning strategies does she or he adopt?

3. From your knowledge of other teachers, select an example of an effective manager and contrast her or him with one you would regard as ineffective. What, in your opinion, distinguishes these two teachers? To what extent do your observations correspond with the differences between effective and ineffective managers identified by research?

4. Half way through term, a child who in the past has not presented any behaviour problems has suddenly lost interest in school work and has started acting aggressively towards other children in the class. How would you cope with this disruption? What kinds of enquiries might you make about the child? What factors might lead you to react differently later? Are the reactions that you can think of now likely to be the ones you would spontaneously make in the classroom? Explain this.

3

Instructional Decision-Making

TEACHING EFFECTIVENESS

THE belief that some teachers or certain ways of teaching are in some sense *more effective* than others has generated much interest and vigorous debate over recent decades. Parents, employers, politicians and others concerned with the products of our schools have questioned, argued, and prescribed (though not necessarily in that order) the type of teaching that is 'best' for pupils. Teachers, teacher trainers and those directly concerned with the practice of teaching have also had to formulate opinions about the nature of good practice and, on occasions, defend their case.

Judgements of effective teaching are obviously required if education is to be guided towards particular goals. But what is an effective teacher? How are such judgements made? Clearly, a judgement of effectiveness presumes certain criteria of good teaching. But in what areas can teachers be expected to have effects or demonstrate excellence? In this there is considerable variation in opinion. On parents' evenings and open days, for example, parents can be heard to voice a variety of expectations about their children's education. Some are concerned more with the social benefits of schooling – how well their children are getting on with other pupils and with teachers. Others are more concerned with their children's satisfaction and enjoyment of school. Still others attach greatest importance to their children's academic progress and potential examination performance. Teachers similarly vary in the aims they hold for education and therefore by implication possess different criteria for judging the effectiveness of teaching (Ashton et al. 1975). Some primary school teachers emphasise the importance of basic skills. Others attach more value to personal development and intellectual autonomy. In reality, of course, people may use several criteria for judging effectiveness (pupils' learning, maturity in attitude and liking of school, for instance).

Our conception of effective or good teaching may, in addition, be complicated by taking into consideration the process by which certain effects are attained. Some teaching processes are in themselves more or less desirable. For example, a teacher whose pupils achieve high examination grades might not be considered a good teacher if these outcomes are attained through devoting a large part of the school day to academic rote-learning, or through an extremely strict system of classroom discipline. Our everyday conceptions of teacher effectiveness are indeed not only varied but also quite complex.

Even when we have established certain criteria, however, judging teacher effectiveness is still problematic. Many of the criteria that people wish to use are in fact difficult to assess. How do we reliably determine whether teachers are encouraging a *willingness to learn*, for example, or developing *intellectual autonomy*? How can such outcomes be identified?

Not surprisingly, everyday talk of teacher effectiveness tends to be somewhat superficial. Judgements of effectiveness are often impressionistic and subjective: they are based upon relatively little information and involve personal criteria of what constitutes good teaching. Consequently, parents may judge a teacher to be effective because their child appears to enjoy school and takes an interest in lessons. The same teacher, however, could be judged ineffective by a teacher colleague who interprets the noise coming from the former's classroom and their lack of emphasis on basic skills as signifying inexperience or incompetence. A teacher can be judged effective by one person's criteria and ineffective by another's. Even the judgements made by one individual may be inconsistent and unreliable due to the sketchy information on which they are often based.

RESEARCH ON TEACHING EFFECTIVENESS

Educational research has for a long time been employed in attempting to make reliable, systematic judgements about the effects of different types of teaching. However, its contribution in this sphere has been somewhat limited. In contrast to the complexity of the concept of effectiveness suggested above, most research has adopted narrow criteria of effectiveness for reasons of practical necessity. Effectiveness studies have tended to focus mostly on the medium-term cognitive outcomes of teaching, a criterion which can be relatively easily and reliably measured and about which there is likely to be a high level of agreement concerning its importance as an educational aim. After all, most people would probably agree that at least one of the important aims of schooling is that pupils master the official curriculum.

Typically, effectiveness studies assess children's performance on attainment tests at the beginning of a school year and then again at the end. This indicates pupils' gains over the period. However, children who already have a large amount of knowledge and skill in a subject area learn more during a year than those who start the year less well prepared. Consequently, the effect of prior learning is eliminated by statistical means before the researcher examines which characteristics of teachers or their teaching appear to account for the remaining levels of pupil achievement.

For a number of reasons, such studies provide us with very crude explanations of teachers' effectiveness. *First*, achievement tests, when designed to be administered to a large number of classes, are necessarily general in nature. They cannot cover the whole year's curriculum in any subject, and since different classes will have experienced somewhat different curricula, the test may assess the achievement of some classes more accurately than others. *Second*, even although certain teacher characteristics or practices may correlate well with pupils' achievement, we cannot be sure that such factors actually caused the achievement. For example, if we found a high correlation between teachers' enthusiasm and children's achievement over the year, this could indeed be due to teachers' enthusiasm in some way influencing the pupils and leading to greater achievement. But alternative explanations *are* possible. Perhaps the children's achievement, caused by some unidentified factor, resulted in the teacher gaining more satisfaction from the work and becoming more enthusiastic; perhaps the children's achievement and the teachers' enthusiasm are both caused by some third factor, such as a set of new, interesting curricular materials or an improvement in classroom facilities. Correlations between teacher characteristics and their pupils' achievement can only provide us with general indications of possible contributors to pupil learning.

Third, one might expect some teachers to be particularly successful in their teaching when dealing with certain types of subject matter, using particular materials, teaching particular types of pupil or in a particular type of school context. A primary school teacher who is effective in teaching the concept of fractions to eight-year-olds or teaching in a school in a predominantly middle-class catchment area may be considerably less effective at teaching creative writing to eleven-year-olds or in teaching in a deprived, inner-city district. Teacher effectiveness studies rarely consider specific activities or topic areas, particular types of children, materials or types of school. Consequently, the only indicators such studies can identify are those general teaching characteristics which relate to effectiveness across broad areas of the curriculum, in several different contexts and with different types of children.

Teacher effectiveness research has developed through various phases (see Medley 1979; Rosenshine 1979). Early studies focussed upon teachers' personality and attitudes as the source of teaching effectiveness, and attempted to relate such features as teachers' 'dominance' and 'affiliation', attributes which were assessed by observation or by using psychological tests, to children's progress in learning. The research led to no consistent findings. Whilst a few studies found relationships between certain aspects of personality and effectiveness, others replicating the research would often find none. The tests used, which were themselves crude measures of personality, were unable to identify consistently any particular personality trait or attitude of the teacher who produced high learning gains.

Later research considered teachers' methods of teaching and ultimately focussed more specifically upon the behaviours (especially the verbal interactions) of teachers while teaching in their own classrooms. In the 1960s and early 1970s when this was a popular style of research, a variety of classroom observation schedules were developed (see Medley and Mitzel 1963, Flanders 1970). These defined a series of teachers' (and sometimes pupils') behaviours, such as 'teacher questions', 'teacher praise', 'teacher lectures'. Schedules or checklists of these behaviours were used by researchers while observing teachers in the classroom. At regular intervals, such as every five seconds, the researcher noted down which category on the schedule best described the teacher's current behaviour. After a few sessions of observation, the resulting data could be used to construct a profile of the teacher's classroom interactions. This would indicate the proportion of observed time that the teacher spent questioning, lecturing, providing feedback, etc. and would provide a summary description of the teacher's behaviour which could then be related to the learning gains of the children in the class.

These studies are referred to as *process-product* studies since they attempt to describe the *process* of teaching (teachers' classroom interactions) and relate it to the *product* of teaching (the learning achieved by the pupils). In contrast to earlier studies they have produced some consistent findings and indicate a style of teaching, labelled *direct teaching* (Rosenshine 1979) which is associated with high learning gains amongst pupils, particularly in basic skills in the primary school, although a few studies have associated this style of teaching with learning gains in the secondary school and also with effective outcomes (children's liking for school work and for the teacher, assessed by attitude questionnaires – see Medley 1979).

Direct teaching is a style of teaching in which teachers ask many questions, closely monitor their pupils' performance and provide frequent and immediate feedback. Direct teaching appears to be academically oriented, and involves considerable control over the content, sequence and structure of classroom activities.

Several researchers have explained the relationship between direct teaching and pupil learning in terms of the amount of time pupils spend involved in classroom work. The longer pupils are involved in basic skills activities, particularly those in which they achieve a high rate of success, the greater are their eventual gains in these areas. Direct teachers, it is argued, maintain a higher level of pupil involvement than others and as a result achieve greater learning gains (Fisher et al. 1981).

However, 'time on task' as it is often called, is essentially a very limited explanation of how teachers' behaviour may influence the learning of their pupils. First, basic skill learning requires the opportunity for memorising new knowledge and practising new skills and consequently it is not surprising that time spent in learning is strongly related to achievement in these areas. However, in other areas of the school curriculum, such as the learning of scientific concepts, where practice and memory play a less significant role and where deeper levels of understanding of subject matter have to be achieved, time spent in learning appears to be much less closely related to pupils' achievement. Second, even in the case of basic skill learning, time alone cannot provide a sufficient explanation for why some children learn more than others. Time can be productively or unproductively used, and what the pupils do during the time they spend in curricular activities would seem crucial in determining the level and extent of their learning. Indeed, Doyle (1979) suggests that time-on-task is strongly correlated to class achievement because the able, motivated pupils generally achieve a lot in class time but low-ability pupils experiencing difficulty do not. The high mean achievements of classes with high rates of on-task behaviour are, he claims, due to the achievements of a minority of able pupils.

Much teacher effectiveness research, process-product studies in particular, has in fact assumed a very simple relationship between teaching and learning. It has been assumed that what teachers do in classrooms *causes* pupil learning. This may seem at first a reasonable claim, yet the relationship between teaching and learning has been demonstrated to be much more complex and interactive.

Teachers are not always in control of what pupils do and learn, for example. Pupils themselves can sometimes determine or negotiate the nature of the activities presented to them. Doyle (1979) describes a strategy which pupils were observed to adopt in order to convert open-ended activities into closed ones. In open activities pupils have no clear indication of right and wrong answers – the activity often requires some creative effort on the pupils' part and is viewed as high-risk. Closed activities on the other hand, have right or wrong answers and are associated with a set of definite expectations from the teacher: these are low-risk activities and, it is suggested, are regarded as less threatening by pupils. Doyle reports instances where pupils renegotiate open activities (free writing, for example) by presenting the teacher with a barrage of questions, 'forcing' the teacher to define the task more precisely, to make her expectations more explicit and to provide cues as to what will be considered a correct or good performance. Consequently, an open-ended activity becomes redefined as a closed one.

Children, in fact, are far from passive recipients of teachers' instruction. Pupils do not automatically attend and perform as the teacher or activity demands. Anderson (1982) found different pupils to be attentive to different extents in different activities. During class discussions with the teacher, some pupils would be actively involved and others would not. Some children were very attentive during oral lessons but tended to spend large portions of time day-dreaming when engaged in individual work using a textbook. Not surprisingly, pupils varied in the extent to which they understood and performed the activity in which they were involved.

Attempting to find out more about pupils' thoughts and perceptions during classroom activities, Swing and Peterson (1982) video-taped lessons in a primary school classroom and later replayed parts of the video-tape to individual pupils who were interviewed about their thoughts at the time. These eleven-year-old children were able to comment about their level of attention to class work, their understanding of the work in progress, and the strategies they adopted to complete it. When the children's performance was assessed using a set of problems related to the lesson, it was found that their reported level of attention, their reported understanding of the lesson and their reported use of certain learning strategies, such as attempting to relate the task demands to previous knowledge, predicted their achievement more accurately than did observers' accounts of the amount of time the pupils spent on the task. What happens inside pupils' heads would seem to reveal more about learning than their overt, observable behaviour.

Recent research provides considerable support for the notion that teaching and learning in the classroom consists of more complex, interactive processes than has been assumed in much effectiveness research. Pupil learning cannot be viewed simply as a consequence of certain teacher behaviours or time spent in classroom activities, for it depends on the attention of the pupils, their understanding of how to perform the required activity, and the strategies they adopt in its performance. Instructionally effective teaching may therefore be more appropriately viewed as involving the continuous assessment of pupils' competencies, the design of activities that will appropriately maintain their attention and result in useful learning, the use of the correct explicative strategies to ensure that pupils can successfully complete them, and monitoring pupils' progress providing feedback and guidance where necessary.

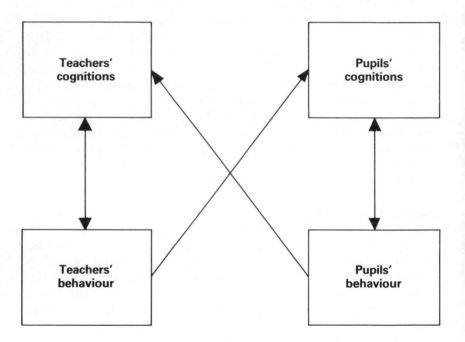

Fig. 3.1 *A cognitive mediational model of teaching and learning.*

The complex, dynamic, interactive nature of teaching and learning can be simply represented in diagram form (see Fig. 3.1). As Shavelson (1973), Winne and Marx (1977) and Doyle (1977) all point out, pupils' states of knowledge, skill and interest are constantly changing, and teachers have to identify and respond to these states in order to promote learning. This representation of teaching is sometimes referred to as the *cognitive mediational model,* since it emphasises the importance of teachers' and pupils' thoughts and decisions as mediators of teaching and learning. Over recent years it has created a change in the nature of teacher effectiveness research. Instead of seeking gross generalisations about the learning gains associated with particular teaching behaviours, research has come to examine the processes by which teachers assess the learning of their pupils, and attempt to influence its development.

TEACHERS' INSTRUCTIONAL DECISION-MAKING

Teachers are engaged in the tasks of designing, implementing and maintaining activities, and it is in the performance of these tasks that teachers make numerous decisions which ultimately influence pupils' learning. But what are these decisions and how do they relate to pupil achievement? At present there is insufficient research to provide a detailed account of the interactive processes involved in classroom teaching and learning, although a number of exploratory studies provide interesting evidence to suggest what some of the decision-making demands upon teachers might be.

DESIGNING ACTIVITIES FOR EFFECTIVE INSTRUCTION

The nature of teacher planning and its curricular context is considered fully in Chapter 4, but several aspects of planning and designing activities must be raised in any discussion of the processes by which teaching helps pupil learning. Many decisions are made in the planning stages of a lesson that determine how activities operate within the classroom and in turn shape children's learning experiences. Decisions concerning the content or subject matter to be covered, the sequencing of the content, the materials to be used and the demands to be placed upon the pupils are of obvious importance.

In some subject areas, knowledge and skills have a clear, hierarchical structure, and decisions concerning the sequencing of activities have important consequences for learning. In arithmetic, the successful performance of some activities depends upon successful learning from earlier ones. Children would have difficulty mastering the multiplication of mixed number fractions, for example, without first mastering the conversion of mixed numbers to improper fractions and the multiplication of simple fractions. The importance of sequencing activities to ensure that pupils have the necessary knowledge and skills to cope with the work presented to them has frequently been asserted. In a series of well-known experiments, Bloom (1976) demonstrated that ensuring children have the required 'entry' knowledge and skills at the beginning of an activity greatly increases their subsequent achievement. Consequently, if teachers are to plan activities which promote learning, they must be aware of the structure of the subject matter and know in which areas their pupils are competent. In practice, teachers frequently entrust decisions regarding the appropriate sequencing of topics to the materials in use, starting at Chapter 1 and working through the book, for instance, or using a structured series of work cards or reading books. McCutcheon (1980), however, warns that teachers should look critically at such materials and consider their appropriateness for the pupils they teach for she suggests that they are sometimes poorly structured and could in some cases even hamper pupil learning.

Zahorik (1982) explored the reasons primary school teachers have for selecting activities and found that teachers often choose those which they expect to arouse greatest interest and attention in their pupils. The fact that activities which result in high levels of pupil involvement are popular with teachers may be because these reduce classroom managerial demands, or perhaps because teachers assume that if the pupils are interested in their work, there is a greater chance that they will learn something from it. In many circumstances this assumption may be quite reasonable, although Zahorik warns that it is important for teachers to distinguish those activities which elicit enthusiasm but present relatively sterile learning opportunities.

Planning decisions concerning the way in which the class is organised for different activities can also influence pupil learning. In case studies of four primary school classrooms, Bossert (1979) found that activities which involved the whole class and in which children's individual performance were public, led to more pupil competition. However, in the classes where children were accustomed to several different activities occurring at once, more co-operation was observed. Obviously, on some occasions it is desirable that children co-operate and learn from one another, but on others, co-operation might be unlikely to yield useful learning, and competition act as a spur to greater achievement. The nature of particular activities and the intentions teachers have for pupil learning may therefore determine how the classroom is most appropriately organised.

Experienced teachers have amassed a vast quantity of knowledge about children in general which is of great value in planning activities.

Even before the year starts, experienced teachers in a sense already 'know' their pupils. Some teachers have taught the same age-range of children, in the same school, with similar curricular materials for several years. They know the kinds of home backgrounds the children have. After teaching older brothers and sisters they sometimes even know the children's families. They know the kinds of experiences the children had prior to school, the kinds of activities they engage in outside school, and teachers of older children are familiar with the curriculum that the pupils have experienced in earlier years. This knowledge is particularly useful to teachers at the beginning of the year before they get to know the individuals in their class. They have an idea of the range of knowledge, skills and interests to expect in their pupils, the likely number of children who will need special help and the types of attitudes, misbehaviours and discipline problems there will be. Teachers also draw upon this knowledge during the year. They recall the problems and difficulties that pupils commonly experience with the materials in use, and they know which topics generally engender or fail to engender, interest. The accumulation of such knowledge enables teachers to plan activities, avoiding or coping in advance with many potential instructional and managerial problems.

Clearly there are many decisions that teachers make in selecting and designing activities which have implications for pupil learning. If such learning is to be more effectively controlled and promoted, teachers need to become aware of these decisions and recognise how they are informed by knowledge of pupils' interests and abilities, the subject matter and classroom organisation.

IMPLEMENTING ACTIVITIES FOR EFFECTIVE INSTRUCTION

The designing of activities provides teachers with a plan for action in the classroom. The plan indicates what teacher and pupils will do, how they will spend their time. Obviously if pupils are to learn from participation in activities, they must attend to the presentation of these activities, understand their demands and become actively involved in them. Teachers engage in various implementation strategies to achieve these ends.

In an interesting study by Winne and Marx (1982), primary school teachers' strategies for engaging pupils in activities were explored. Lessons were video-taped and later replayed to the teachers, who were instructed to stop the video-tape at points where they were aware of

attempting to influence pupils' thinking. In addition, segments of the
video-tape were also replayed to pupils who were interviewed about
their thoughts at these times. Winne and Marx identified three broad
areas of strategy which describe teachers' attempts to influence the
thinking of pupils.

First, teachers engaged in *orienting*, or controlling the focus of pupils'
attention. Lessons frequently started with the teacher attempting to
arouse enthusiasm for the coming activity. Teachers would also identify
and signal to pupils the content to be learned or the information to be
attended to, and cue the pupils into the procedures for acquiring the
necessary information. *Orienting* was basically concerned with introducing an activity, but could also occur later in lessons when teachers were
aware of pupils losing interest or experiencing difficulty with the
activity. Teachers could be orienting pupils to an activity when they say,
for example, 'Barry, what did we say last week about surface tension?'
or 'Right, today we are having a test'.

Second, teachers would communicate, often through demonstration,
the *cognitive processing* that the activity required. Different types of
activity require different types of *cognitive processing* or mental
operations. Creative writing, for example, requires the generation of
original ideas and expression, whereas mathematical activities frequently involve the manipulation of information according to a specific set of
rules which the pupil may be expected to remember. Teachers may
demonstrate examples on the blackboard to attempt to signal to pupils
the cognitive processing in which they are expected to engage. Winne
and Marx found that teachers not only explained the demands of the
activity at the beginning of the lessons, but also frequently checked that
pupils had understood these demands by questioning them or providing
rules or procedures by which they could check their own performance.

Third, after pupils had mastered certain content or procedures,
teachers would sometimes attempt to influence their learning through
consolidation, providing further practice so that knowledge might be
more readily called to mind (as in the case of arithmetic tables or
spelling, for instance) or that skills might become fluent (as in the case
of handwriting or gymnastics). Practice sessions and drills are a familiar
feature of primary schools where there are a number of basic skills and
areas of knowledge that have to be readily brought into use. These drills
or rehearsals can occur at the beginning of activities when they serve to
ensure that pupils remember the required knowledge and skill, but oral
drills are also used during and at the end of activities to provide
feedback or review progress.

The importance to the learner of *orienting*, identifying *cognitive
processing* and *consolidation* becomes apparent if we return to the

example of learning to drive a car. When first learning to drive we have to be told which cues to attend to (orienting) and how to use this information (cognitive processing). We are instructed, for example, to note the line of the kerb in relation to our view of the bonnet and thereby judge the position of the car on the road. We also need practice in order to develop these skills (consolidation). It is through the use of such strategies that teachers appear to influence pupils' learning and performance of activities.

MAINTAINING ACTIVITIES FOR EFFECTIVE INSTRUCTION

Maintaining a committed, constructive involvement in classroom activities is an important aspect of teaching which is both managerial and instructional in nature. Teachers possess repertoires of general managerial routines for maintaining pupil attention to task and minimising disruption, as discussed in Chapter 2. However, keeping pupils effectively engaged in activities so that learning as opposed to simply 'busyness' takes place may also depend upon a number of more specific instructional strategies. In particular, teachers, in order to maintain pupils' interest in activities and to ensure successful performance, have to make frequent assessments of pupils' work and provide feedback. Studies of different types of feedback on pupil performance have repeatedly affirmed its importance in promoting pupil learning, particularly that which points out errors in understanding or performance and directs pupils to successful completion (Kulhavy 1977).

Experienced teachers can have a vast repertoire of diagnostic/ remediation *routines*. While teaching particular lessons, teachers have been found to be attuned to particular difficulties which they readily identify and respond to automatically (Leinhardt 1982, Calderhead 1983). In teaching a lesson on the division of fractions, for example, a teacher may be primed to notice certain errors in the pupils' work, such as forgetting to invert the divisor, incorrectly changing mixed fractions and mistakes in 'cancelling down', and may respond to these with a routine instructional response. Similarly, in a creative writing lesson, a teacher may be attuned to finding children who lack ideas, children whose writing consists of a series of brief statements connected with a string of *ands* and *thens*, or various errors of grammar, spelling and punctuation that are thought to warrant correction.

Leinhardt (1982) uses the term *agenda* to refer to the knowledge which teachers have readily available for reference during the lesson or the day's teaching. Leinhardt suggests that teachers continually revise and update their agenda, so that they are prepared to cope with the situations they are likely to confront in the immediate future.

As well as instructional routines, Leinhardt suggests that teachers' agendas also include knowledge about pupils which may be relevant to the teaching process. This knowledge may consist of pupils' general characteristics as well as some more specific details of learning difficulties. A study of teachers' commentaries upon their classroom behaviour in fact found that teachers' routine responses to some classroom difficulties are often influenced more by teachers' general perceptions of the pupils than by the nature of the difficulty itself (Calderhead 1983). For example, when a pupil approaches the teacher with a particular problem, the situation could be interpreted in such terms as the child being careless, seeking attention, having an 'off-day' or the work being too difficult. Which interpretation teachers placed upon the event was found often to depend upon the teachers' knowledge of the child. One teacher, for example, was observed to spend several minutes helping a child with an arithmetic problem by asking a series of helpful questions and guiding the child through the process by which he would achieve the answer, yet later to send another child with the same problem back to his seat to puzzle it out for himself. As the teacher explained afterwards, she did not expect the former child to be able to cope with the problem on his own, whereas she judged the latter child to be able but not trying.

The routines that teachers have for responding to pupil difficulty, providing feedback and guiding pupils through classroom activities, can be responsive to complex configurations of cues, and can take both managerial and instructional considerations into account. Hoffman and Kugle (1982) for example, point out that when dealing with pupils' reading difficulties, infant teachers frequently respond to features of the child, the difficulty, the materials and the classroom context, as noted in Chapter 1.

In maintaining pupils' constructive involvement in activities, teachers face a demanding task. The repertoire of instructional and managerial routines with which teachers approach this task and the facility with which they are used, are clearly important influences upon the learning of their pupils.

IMPEDIMENTS TO INSTRUCTIONAL EFFECTIVENESS

It may seem somewhat self-evident that instruction is likely to be effective if teachers know their pupils, their subject matter and the business of classroom organisation well, and if they are able to design and implement activities which are (1) well matched to their pupils' existing knowledge and skills, (2) which provide opportunities for further development and (3) which are well-managed (involving feedback where appropriate) to ensure productive performance. However, such practice is not typical. If we were to observe what happens in our schools, we would quickly find examples of activities which for pupils are unproductive and even demotivating. It is not uncommon, for instance, to find pupils spending large amounts of time copying notes from a book or a blackboard or completing exercises in which they have already well-mastered the relevant knowledge and skills.

Obviously, not all time in schools can be spent teaching and learning. It would probably not be humanly possible for either teacher or pupils to be so engaged for six hours a day, five days a week. Some activities, particularly in the primary school, may not even be intended to promote learning, but are done for fun, or as light relief for pupils and teacher during the course of the day. However, there are many examples where potential learning experiences have become substituted with 'busyness'. Literature reporting classroom observations abounds with examples where the teacher has become concerned with keeping the class occupied or busy, rather than learning (Holt 1969, Sharp and Green 1975, Woods 1979). For some teachers, it would seem that management has become an end in itself and instruction has become of relatively minor importance.

Various obstacles make it difficult for teachers to promote efficient learning in the classroom. Principal among these are the number and variety of pupils in the class. When confronted with pupils of various backgrounds, experience and abilities, it is not surprising that teachers sometimes find their instructions and explanations are understood or misunderstood in numerous different ways. Winne and Marx (1982) point out the frequent mismatch between the intentions teachers have for some of their instructional behaviour and the ways in which pupils interpret it. For example, one of their teachers started a lesson outlining an activity and stating what he expected pupils to achieve by the end, with the intention of arousing enthusiasm. However, this was interpreted by one pupil as an attempt to make the task easier, and by another as the teacher making the pupils anxious, for the task, which involved measuring the height of a tree, seemed difficult!

In a study of mathematics and language work in primary schools, Bennett and Desforges (1984) estimated that just over half of all classroom tasks were poorly matched to the abilities of the pupils. Less able children tended to be given work that was too difficult for them and able children work that was too easy. Teachers were often aware of the former occasions – slow completion rates or pupils' errors clearly signalled this – although they often seemed to accept the situation as inevitable. However, teachers were not able to identify occasions when the work was too easy. It is suggested that the 'signals' for this are not so readily visible.

Because of the managerial demands upon teachers in classrooms where they may be controlling several activities at once, it is often impossible for them to check individual pupils' interpretations of instructions and what the pupils understand the nature of their activity to be. Instead of meeting learning difficulties with investigation and remedial help, teachers have sometimes developed strategies which ignore the learning problem or leave the child to develop appropriate knowledge and skills through trial and error. Such strategies are brought to light in a study by Rohrkemper and Brophy (1983) in which 98 primary teachers were given descriptions of pupils who had difficulties with their work. For example, one description was of a child called Joe:

> Joe could be a capable student, but his self-concept is so poor that he actually describes himself as stupid. He makes no serious effort to learn, shrugging off responsibility by saying that 'that stuff' is too hard for him. Right now he is dawdling instead of getting started on an assignment you know he can do. You know that if you approach him, he will begin to complain that the assignment is too hard and that he can't do it.

The teachers were asked to imagine these pupils in the context of their own classroom, to talk about pupil and incident and say how they would cope. In the case of Joe, most of the teachers viewed the problem as primarily a motivational one and claimed that they would respond with praise and encouragement, and would provide him with some help to get started. Less than 20 per cent of the teachers thought that Joe's problem might involve learning difficulties. In these cases, the teachers claimed that they would re-explain the activity to Joe, 'walk' him through several related problems, check that he could do them and possibly change the activity to one which would better suit his knowledge and abilities.

Such reactions were common across several pupil descriptions. Teachers generally responded to inattention with a motivating or disciplinary response, without considering the possibility that it might be the outcome of learning difficulties.

Although this research took place in an artificial context, the teachers' classes were also observed prior to this exercise to assess whether in reality teachers responded to similar situations in the ways they described. The researchers felt that their observations generally validated the teachers' reported strategies.

Similar evidence is also reported from a classroom observational study by Anderson (1982), who suggests that teachers could deal with pupils' inattention much more constructively. She recommends, for example, that teachers consider changing the nature of a group activity to make an inattentive pupil more involved in it, ensuring that children's attention is not distracted or interrupted, and encouraging children more positively to seek help when they are in difficulty or to check their understanding of an activity when in doubt.

Given that children may occasionally, or even frequently, be left to resolve their own learning difficulties, it is not surprising that they sometimes develop completely erroneous notions of how to complete activities. From case studies of children in mathematics classes, Erlwanger (1975) describes children who have developed arithmetical procedures that are quite inappropriate but which on some occasions provide by chance a right answer. Other children were found to have learned appropriate procedures but to lack any understanding of their meaning. One child could competently cancel twenty-thirty-fifths to four-sevenths, for example, but thought the former was larger because it had more pieces. Similarly, Anderson and Brubaker (1983) in a study of several primary school classes, suggest that low-ability children in particular seem to learn a variety of erroneous procedures for doing their work.

Studies of children in classrooms suggest that pupils can often regard the object of activities as coming up with right answers as opposed to learning, and, in some cases, this concern predominates their thinking. In one class of ten-year-olds, for example, a teacher was observed to spend half an hour introducing the notion of proportion. She read out various problems of the type: 'three men build a wall in six days, how long would it take two men to build the same wall?' After each question, she systematically guided the class through a series of stages: What was the question asking them to find out? What information did the question give? How could the information help answer the question? At each stage the teacher used the blackboard to record the relevant information or to perform the appropriate calculation. At the end of the lesson, the teacher explained to the author that she had wanted the children to think about the questions and to puzzle out how the information given was to be used to find the answer, hoping that children might 'latch on to such concepts as "man-hours"'. Interestingly, when twelve of the children in the class were interviewed about their perceptions of the lesson, only one shared the same perception as the teacher. The others viewed the lesson as being concerned with demonstrating how to set out 'the workings' of proportion problems in their notebooks. It seemed that, although not directed by the teacher to do so, the pupils had mostly attended to the procedure for getting the right answer and how to 'set it out'. In this case, the pupils' strategy could have been due to the fact that proportion problems are difficult for most ten-year-olds, and after failing to understand the teachers' explanations, they may have adopted the next best strategy of memorising how to cope with them. Alternatively, it may have been due to a general learned strategy on the part of the pupils – finding out how to produce right answers.

In some cases, the need to produce right answers and an inability to alleviate their own learning difficulties can lead children to develop various cheating strategies. Most classrooms probably involve some level of illicit 'co-operation'. On occasion, teachers may even decide to ignore this as long as it doesn't occur too often, since it could be very time-consuming to eliminate completely. On other occasions, however, it can become a major problem, especially when it goes unnoticed by the teacher.

In one rather exceptional case observed by the author, a junior school class demonstrated considerable ingenuity in their strategies for using an SRA reading laboratory. The whole class worked on the activity at the same time, and there were numerous established procedures for obtaining the cards, noting the time taken to complete each card, and marking the work. These procedures were obviously aimed at preventing long queues at the SRA box, or at the teacher's desk. During the activity, the teacher stressed that the pupils should attempt to solve problems on their own, and only come out for help if they were 'really, really stuck'. This again helped to reduce demands upon the teacher's time. However, the necessity to resolve their own problems, added to the competitiveness of the activity (a mark of 100 per cent three times in succession allowed them to progress to the next colour), and the teacher's surprisingly low level of vigilance, resulted in a variety of devious ploys.

Trades would be done between children sitting in the same group who were working on the same colour (level) so that they would each choose a work card for which the other could already provide the answers. One child had developed an ingenious strategy of taking the answer card not for the work card he had just completed but for the one he would select on the next occasion and noting down the answers for future reference! The teacher insisted on the pupils showing her their workbook before taking an answer card and again after they had marked it, but the pupils seemed to have quickly grasped that on the first occasion this would be a cursory glance to ensure that no blanks had been left for answers to be put in later, and that on the second the teacher would spot answers that had been rubbed out or otherwise changed. Nevertheless, at least one child had found a way of beating the system. When he came to multiple-choice questions requiring an A, B, C response, if unsure of the correct answer he would write C but in such a way that the bottom curve of the C was not fully formed. When he later obtained the answer card he would then easily convert his partly formed C into A, B or a fully formed C without incurring suspicion. In this class, although the teacher was aware of the possibilities of cheating and sometimes caught pupils out, she was so engaged in managing the activity that many of the cheating strategies went completely unnoticed.

Teachers, however, do make several efforts to cater more appropriately for the different abilities within their classes. *Grouping* is one common practice in primary schools where, in different subject areas, pupils will be grouped and taught according to their attainment. Another common practice is to use *curriculum packages* which allow children to work at different levels and rates often using workcards or graded workbooks (e.g. the many primary maths schemes such as SMP or Fletcher). Little is known about the effectiveness of these efforts in promoting greater learning. Unfortunately, their benefits do have to be weighed against a number of apparent disadvantages. By grouping children to work at different levels and rates often using work cards or graded workbooks (e.g. the many primary maths schemes such as SMP quote Pluckrose (see Silberman 1973) the teacher can become like an expert juggler trying to keep thirty different plates in the air. The use of maths packages in primary schools, for example, is often accompanied by long queues at the teacher's desk where children want terms explained, problems solved or simply to know the whereabouts of a piece of mathematical equipment which is required for the next problem. Certainly, teachers can attempt to minimise these demands, by providing a subject table, for example, with all the necessary materials available on it. But even in an efficiently organised classroom, the managerial demands are high. Thirty children working on separate activities inevitably ensures a steady stream of problems and materials that aren't always where they should be! Primary maths packages are generally intended to be accompanied by various mathematical games or activities in which the teacher helps the children who are working at a particular level to understand the necessary concepts and procedures involved in the work they are about to do. For example, the topic of co-ordinates might be introduced with a game in which the children stand on different floor tiles in the classroom and have to work out the number of tiles in each direction that they would have to move across in order to reach one of the other children. However, such activities may often be left out of the mathematics curriculum simply because the teacher's time is wholly involved in keeping individual activities going. How the use of such materials influences the amount of instruction and management the teacher engages in and how this is reflected in pupils' learning obviously deserves much fuller study.

Teaching children in groups, particularly if formed according to their abilities, might also have some undesirable side-effects not only in terms of increasing the amount of time teachers spend in management, but in restricting the learning that occurs through interaction with children of different abilities and through observing these children in interaction with the teacher. Morine-Dershimer (1982) for example, found that when pupils hear other children being praised by the teacher, this is often interpreted as a signal – an indication of the demands of the activity or the teacher's expectations. Pupils were found to tune in to a variety of cues concerning other children's performance and the teacher's response to it. This provided a means of assessing the expectations for their own performance. Certainly, when children work in small groups the scope for obtaining such cues must be somewhat reduced. Filby and Barnett (1982) similarly point out that when reading is taught in small homogeneous groups, children have no opportunity of listening to readers of different abilities. The less able readers, in particular, are therefore deprived of a source of cues about the nature of competent reading. Swing and Peterson (1982) also suggest that heterogeneous groups, particularly those in which children are encouraged to help one another, may have considerable learning benefits, particularly for the lower-ability pupils. However, the effects of different grouping policies on classroom interaction and learning are still not fully understood, and a variety of factors would seem to determine whether or not groups contribute to pupil achievement (see Webb 1982).

Teachers are faced with the task of instructing pupils within a complex context. A variety of factors can interfere with the instructional process, and attempts to improve the quality of pupils' learning experiences can clearly have quite unpredictable consequences. In addition, it has also to be remembered that in the classroom teachers are involved in more than simply instruction. They have to maintain order in the classroom and teachers may also regard it as important to develop a pleasant working environment and so encourage good relationships with the children. These various functions which teachers aim to fulfil may well conflict at times. For example, when teachers provide feedback to pupils after an activity, their concern is probably not solely with improving performance, but also with the motivation of the pupils and the pupils' own self-concepts. The feedback which seems to be the most constructive may also be the most demoralising. Consequently, teachers' apparently instructional strategies may on occasions be serving a multiplicity of functions, taking into account more than simply instructional factors. The business of instruction is embedded in the total life of the classroom.

IMPLICATIONS FOR INSTRUCTIONAL EFFECTIVENESS

It is difficult to make firm recommendations for instruction that might lead to improved learning, since much of the research in the area is exploratory and in need of replication and extension. At present there are more questions raised about instructional effectiveness than have been answered.

Most of the research on the effects of teaching upon learning has been conducted with primary school teachers and pupils. Secondary schools have some special characteristics, such as subject specialisms and an examinations-oriented curriculum, which one would expect to influence instructional processes. Nevertheless, there are sufficient similarities in the teaching of both institutions, and the tentative suggestions to arise from research are of such a general nature, that they could probably be usefully considered in either context.

First, it would seem valuable for teachers to be more aware of the demands of the activities they establish in the classroom, to analyse the tasks they provide pupils in terms of the knowledge and skills they require and the procedures they involve, and to consider whether the pupils in fact possess these. For example, in planning a creative writing lesson on an unfamiliar topic, a teacher might consider what a successfully completed essay would look like, and then consider whether the pupils possess the vocabulary, the motivation, the imagery and the mastery of writing conventions to produce this, before deciding the instructional inputs that would be necessary for the pupils to make a reasonable try.

In some cases, when a child has difficulty with a task, a deeper analysis than this may be helpful. For example, telling the time requires a large number of specific competencies – being able to identify the 'big' hand and the 'little' hand, understanding what they represent and the relationship between minutes and hours, knowing how the hands move on a conventional clock, being able to identify 'o'clock' positions, etc. By breaking the task down into specific competencies, it becomes possible for teachers to appreciate the knowledge and skills demanded and to identify those areas in which a child experiencing difficulty requires remedial help. Analyses of activities might in fact help teachers appreciate more fully the learning problems their pupils experience.

Second, it is clear that even when teachers have explained an activity and how it is to be performed, pupils can adopt inappropriate strategies and fail to engage in useful learning. Ideally, teachers need to be able to monitor the thinking processes of each of their pupils to check whether they have understood and are employing appropriate procedures. Obviously, this is not possible in a conventional classroom, but much can be gained from close observation, from working through examples with the child, or by asking the child how they go about the activity and listening to their description. Many of the difficulties encountered by pupils could be easily spotted by teachers if they had the time and could arrange to observe their pupils at work more closely. In going some way towards this, teachers may find it profitable to approach the observation of pupils more systematically. For example, in a normal teaching context, it may be possible to select one child per day for close observation. Alternatively, a team-teaching arrangement in which one teacher takes on the routine management of the class while the other monitors particular pupils' performance and provides the required remedial help may provide a solution. Or teachers might arrange to spend brief periods, observing one another's classes if they have the time available. Teachers seconded for higher degree courses who spend part of this time observing classrooms have an excellent opportunity of course to study pupils at work. Such experiences have led to an awareness of pupils' strategies that is useful on returning to the classroom.

Last, teachers' instructional function has to be carried out in a complex environment. Though no ready solutions can be offered, it would seem important that teachers attempt to understand how their own actions interact with the contexts in which they work to mould the learning experiences of their pupils. The strategies of teachers to improve children's learning may not always take effect as expected and such strategies may continue to be unproductive until the problem is interpreted in terms of the wider learning context of the classroom. Only careful observation and evaluation can help teachers understand more fully the instructional processes at work.

This chapter has focused on the processes of instruction, but teaching of course is not concerned only with instruction. Teachers are viewed, and view themselves, as fulfilling a number of other functions. In children's lives, teachers often play an important role and their influence undoubtedly extends far beyond formal learning. For both pupils and teachers, school is part of a way of life, and in the process of schooling, attitudes and relationships are formed as well as knowledge and skills gained. Nevertheless, teaching the curriculum is an important part of teachers' work, and this could be made more efficient and rewarding to children. Teachers would be in a position to promote greater achievement if they could understand better how their own actions relate to pupil learning. Such an understanding would seem to be a promising outcome of much more detailed investigation of the thinking of teachers and pupils in classrooms.

RECOMMENDED READING

Armstrong, M (1980) *Closely Observed Children*. London: Writers and Readers.
An observational study of children learning in an informal Leicestershire primary school. It describes in detail how children's interests lead them into particular learning situations and how their learning develops in the context of particular activities. It also provides interesting material for discussion on how teachers might most appropriately structure the classroom environment, and aim to foster pupils' learning.

The Elementary School Journal
Two *special issues* of this journal are of particular interest. 'Students in classrooms', **82**(5), 1982 focuses on students' experiences in classrooms, with several papers on pupils' thinking. 'Research on teaching' **83**(4), 1983 contains review papers on pupils' perceptions of schooling and research on instructional effectiveness.

EXERCISES

1. Examine an activity (e.g. drawing a map, or working on a particular textbook exercise) that you might present to your class, or one that you have observed in another teacher's class. Specify the knowledge and skill that the activity demands. How could you check beforehand that the pupils have the necessary knowledge and skill to cope with the activity? What would you expect the children to learn from the activity?
2. Observe a teacher introducing a new activity. What steps are taken to (a) interest the pupils, (b) cue the pupils in to relevant information, (c) communicate the nature of the activity, (d) check that the pupils understand the activity and have the knowledge and skills to complete it? Once the pupils have started the activity, talk to some of them about their work. Have they understood the nature of the activity? Are they

performing it correctly? What are they learning? How would you improve upon the teaching in a subsequent lesson with similar children?

3. Observe a pupil who is experiencing difficulty with class work. Talk to them about the activity they are engaged in. How do they perceive the activity? Have they understood the activity correctly? Do they possess the necessary knowledge and skill to complete it? What is the nature of the child's difficulty? Suggest some remedial strategies that might be appropriate and discuss these with your tutor.

4. Taking one regular classroom activity with which you are familiar, consider the constraints which might influence how teachers design, implement and maintain the activity. How might these constraints ultimately influence pupils' learning?

5. Observe two or three children during the course of a lesson. How much time do they spend (a) interacting with the teacher (b) interacting with other children (c) working on their own (d) wasting time (standing in queues, for example)?* If you can hear pupils' interactions, describe what they talk about during the activity – is it related to the activity or not? What kind of help, if any, is obtained from the teacher and from other pupils? Describe the nature of the activity and what the children did. From your observations and talking to the children afterwards, describe what you think the children learned from the lesson.

---

*A checklist of these four categories on which the category matching the current pupil behaviour is ticked once every twenty seconds, over a period of about twenty minutes, may be helpful in this estimation.

4
Teachers' Planning

PLANNING is a vital though often undervalued aspect of classroom teaching. Although teachers spend much of their professional time in face-to-face interactions with pupils in the classroom where the business of teaching and learning is seen to take place, the nature and effects of classroom processes are often largely determined by the efforts of teachers beforehand in the less frequently observed processes of preparation and design. As indicated in Chapters 2 and 3, planning makes important contributions to classroom management and instruction. In addition, it is in planning that teachers translate syllabus guidelines, institutional expectations and their own beliefs and ideologies of education into guides for action in the classroom. This aspect of teaching provides the structure and purpose for what teachers and pupils do in the classroom. In any examination of classroom practice, it is therefore important to consider the nature of teacher planning, its context and its effects.

TRADITIONAL PRESCRIPTIONS FOR PLANNING

Until recently most of the writing about instructional planning has been prescriptive in orientation. The concern of educationalists has been with how lessons, courses and the school curriculum *ought* to be planned. Little attention was given to what teachers actually did when they planned, or for that matter what was possible for them to do. Theorists such as Tyler (1949) and Wheeler (1967) adopted an analytical approach to planning, and suggested that it consists of a number of sequential decisions. They reasoned that since teaching is a purposeful, goal-directed activity, the essential starting point for planning is the selection of educational aims and objectives. Aims were commonly considered to be general statements of purpose (e.g. 'to develop basic numeracy') whereas objectives were more specific expressions of aims (e.g. 'to develop mastery of the procedures for the addition of two single-digit numerals'). The planning of a school curriculum or of a particular course would therefore start with a listing of *aims* and their breakdown into more specific objectives which could be attributed to units of a course or individual lessons. Second, the *content* of lessons would be decided – what educational experiences would be likely to achieve these objectives? Third, decisions would be made about *organisation* – how is the content best presented to facilitate the achievement of the chosen objectives? Lastly, it was suggested that teachers *evaluate* their lessons, and assess the extent to which objectives have been achieved and that this information be used to guide future instruction.

Several theorists have produced similar analytical accounts of the planning in which it is thought teachers ought to engage, and these are frequently referred to as *objective models* or *rational planning models*. Critics of such models (Eisner 1967, Stenhouse 1975) have raised a number of objections. For example, some areas of the curriculum, such as creative writing or English literature, cannot be readily analysed in terms of objectives. Teachers may also hold different objectives for different pupils as opposed to objectives for a particular lesson or course. In addition, it was questioned whether the time teachers spend thinking about objectives is in fact repaid in terms of more effective teaching and learning. Despite criticisms, objective models have had a powerful influence in the design of some curricula. Many of the teachers' handbooks which accompany classroom materials or the textbooks which teachers use begin with a long list of objectives around which the materials have been designed. Teachers are also sometimes encouraged either in their training or in their schools, to start lesson planning by stating the objectives to be achieved.

Certainly, there are arguments to be made for teachers thinking about instructional objectives. It may encourage them to consider the intended effects of their teaching and the extent to which these are being achieved. An awareness of specific objectives may in some cases help teachers to structure pupils' learning experience and become more aware of their pupils' learning progress. However, those who have experienced planning in accordance with an objectives model will no doubt have realised that in practice it rarely operates as intended. Student teachers, for example, in writing up their lesson plans in the 'objective–content–organisation–evaluation' format, frequently confess to deciding the content and organisation of their lesson first, then deciding afterwards upon the objectives to be achieved – often wording them in such a way as might please their tutor! Indeed, it has been suggested that a very similar practice has been adopted by curriculum developers in some supposedly objectives-oriented texts! (See Brown and McIntyre 1982.)

If the objectives model does not adequately describe teachers' normal practice, and if this approach to planning has not in reality been widely adopted, how then do teachers plan and what effects do teachers' own planning procedures have?

RESEARCH ON TEACHERS' PLANNING

If planning is defined in terms of the preparations that teachers make for teaching, it can clearly encompass a wide range of activities. It can include making special materials for a lesson, taking part in school curriculum meetings, reading books to become familiar with particular subject matter, drafting out a department syllabus, keeping a record of daily work plans, conferring with colleagues over team-teaching arrangements, reading teachers' handbooks, selecting exercises from textbooks, or even simply thinking about what needs to be revised in tomorrow's arithmetic lesson or considering what topic might be chosen for the pupils' next essay.

Because planning involves such a diverse range of activities which are pursued throughout the year both in and out of school, it is difficult to estimate how much time it in fact demands of teachers, and how all this time is used. A US survey of primary school teachers suggests that they spend an average of about two hours per day on planning, although this varies considerably from one teacher to another (Clark and Yinger 1980). Several investigations (Morine 1976, Yinger 1980, McCutcheon 1980) have suggested that most of the planning in which teachers engage is fairly informal – *mental planning*, as McCutcheon terms it. Contrary to the popular notion of teaching being a 9-to-4 job, teachers, it is noted, frequently think about their work outside school hours. Sometimes this involves a period of systematic planning and thinking about the next day's lessons, but it more frequently consists of snatching odd moments for reflection about teaching at times when their minds are not fully occupied with other things. In fact, some aspects of teachers' planning seem to be commonly accomplished while having a bath, eating breakfast or driving to work in the morning!

Investigations of teachers' planning have employed a number of different methods to describe the processes involved. Course planning has been investigated by observing staff discussions on course development, interviewing individual members of staff and by questionnaires. Teachers have also been observed when they plan individual lessons and their overt behaviours, such as referring to books or making brief notes, recorded. In some studies, teachers have planned lessons 'aloud', verbalising their normally covert thought processes which have been tape-recorded and later analysed. Other studies have relied upon interviewing teachers about their planning either of particular lessons or of their classroom work in general.

Not surprisingly, most of teachers' planning has been found to focus on the preparation of particular lessons. For these, teachers rarely produce sophisticated written plans, though McCutcheon found that brief notes and 'memory joggers' were common, and would generally involve a listing of the topics to be covered, or the books to be used and exercises to be done. For example, one teacher's written plan for part of a day's work looked like this:

Reading
Group 1 Read pp. 57–63. Discuss? in TG p. 187. Workbook pp. 12–13 suffixes. Boardwork – suffixes, TG p. 188–189.
Social studies
Map reading. Dittos of Magellan's and da Gama's voyages. Groups put on project maps or project globe. Discuss oceans and continents.

Studies of teachers' thinking during lesson planning (Zahorik 1975, Morine 1976, Peterson, Marx and Clark 1978, Yinger 1979) reveal a wide range of concerns. On some occasions, teachers' thoughts focus on the preparation of materials, on others they are preoccupied with deciding how to cope with particular pupil difficulties, and on others they may be concerned with a mental rehearsal and evaluation of alternative explanations or demonstrations. In general, however, when planning lessons, teachers' thinking has been found to concern mostly the subject matter to be covered, their pupils' abilities and possible reactions to the subject matter and what they wish the pupils to do. Planning is aimed principally at the selection or construction of *activities*. Some researchers have referred to activities as 'controlled behaviour settings' (e.g. Yinger 1980) since they serve to define how teachers and pupils will behave during the lesson in a particular classroom context. Activities are understood by teachers, and also by pupils when they are a common part of classroom life, as defining certain classroom processes. 'Spelling', 'arithmetic' or 'project', for example, may signify certain expectations for how the classroom will operate and what the teacher and pupils will do.

In designing an activity, teachers consider a number of factors and make several decisions. They may have to decide on the subject matter to be covered, the information to be given to pupils, the procedures to be demonstrated, the books and materials to be used, or the exercises to be adopted. These decisions, however, must also take into consideration features of the context in which the teacher works – the selection of resources available, the abilities and interests of the pupils, the syllabus and possibly a variety of other factors, such as school policy and timetabling restrictions.

Designing activities basically involves such issues as what is going to be done, by whom, when, where, with what materials and with what level of assistance from the teacher, how the work is to be accomplished, and the expectations that should be held for pupil behaviour during the activity. And these decisions must obviously take account of the context in which teachers find themselves.

Experienced teachers, however, have various 'plans-in-memory' (Olson 1982) as a result of their previous experiences and may rarely need to design an activity from scratch. Planning may revolve largely around thinking about how a similar lesson 'went down' on a previous occasion, and making a few appropriate adjustments to the mental plan. In addition, some activities have become a routine part of classroom life. Teachers may simply plan to do 'arithmetic' or 'reading' and the only thinking necessary may be to consider which is the appropriate exercise and even that is sometimes largely determined by the books or materials in use.

For beginning teachers, however, the designing of an activity may warrant much more thinking. Furthermore, beginning teachers are often handicapped by a lack of appropriate knowledge. They may be unfamiliar with the pupils they are about to teach, the materials in use and have few past experiences from which to extract suggestions for future practice. Consequently, it is not surprising that beginning teachers' planning has generally been found to be fairly superficial. Ben-Peretz (1981) for example, in comparing the reported planning thoughts of experienced teachers and student teachers on the same lesson topic, found that experienced teachers' planning protocols were longer than the students' and made much more specific references to the subject matter, pupils and classroom organisation. This supports an earlier finding by Joyce and Harootunian (1968) who interviewed a group of student teachers after each had planned a science lesson. The researchers observed that students' plans were generally brief and crude and not clearly thought out. Joyce and Harootunian suggest that students, when planning lessons, think about what they have observed in other teachers' classrooms, and generally aim to replicate the classroom practice which they have witnessed and remembered.

Neither experienced teachers nor student teachers have been found to think very much about objectives. In Zahorik's (1975) study, 194 teachers, drawn from the primary, secondary and further education sectors were all asked to note down the decisions they made as they planned a lesson and to note the order in which they made them. 51 per cent started with a decision concerning *content*. The most common decision concerned *activities* (81 per cent). Only 28 per cent started their planning with a decision concerning *objectives*. The same trends were found irrespective of the subject or the age of pupils taught. McCutcheon (1980) found that, of 24 primary teachers whose planning was studied, objectives tended only to be mentioned when the teachers were required to note these down as part of school policy. When questioned about their lack of use of objectives, teachers pointed out that obviously all school work has objectives in the sense that it is intended to achieve something, but objectives were written at the beginning of textbooks or in teachers' manuals; they were implicit in the exercises and the materials that were used, but they didn't see any point in thinking about them or writing them down. It was felt that teachers' selection of activities depended largely upon the children involved and the materials available, and these were the factors that teachers had to consider most.

Research on teachers' planning suggests that teachers engage in a process that contrasts sharply with the prescribed rational planning model. Whereas the prescribed model starts with a statement of aims and objectives, followed by a reasoning of the content and organisation to be adopted and how the pupils' performance is to be evaluated to assess whether the objectives have been achieved, teachers' plans reflect little concern either with objectives or with evaluations. In reality, the process of planning seems to be more appropriately conceptualised as a problem-solving process. Teachers, faced with a variety of factors such as pupils with certain knowledge, abilities and interests, the availability of particular textbooks and materials, the syllabus, the timetable, the expectations of headteachers and others, and their own knowledge of previous teaching encounters, *have to solve the problem of how to structure the time and experiences of pupils in the classroom*. Teachers, it seems, adopt a much more pragmatic approach than that prescribed for curriculum design. Rather than start with a conception of what is to be achieved and deduce which classroom activities would therefore be ideal, teachers start with a conception of their working context and from that decide what is possible.

This is illustrated in the following account of planning provided by a junior school teacher. It was given in response to a request to describe her planning for the following day's work and therefore it includes explanations that would not normally enter into her planning thoughts and probably excludes some of the more detailed thoughts (about particular exercises to be covered, etc.) that might occur when the teacher plans alone. However, the account illustrates the common concerns of teachers in planning, the obstacles around which they plan, and the types of routine activities that teachers often rely upon.

> We always start the day with a discussion of what is happening in the news. You see the children take it in turns to bring in a clipping from the papers. Each group brings in one piece of news and they either read it out or talk about it. If it's something interesting it sometimes stimulates a debate... That usually takes us up to half past nine, or sometimes a bit later if they really get going. It might be shorter tomorrow though because I said I was going to miss one group out – because they were being silly about their news today. After that, we'll do mental arithmetic: they all do the same work apart from the two remedial children – they work from a separate book, and they usually need some help to get started. The rest of the class will know what to do – we follow the exercises in the book. They mark their own work from the answer books and I check to see how they've got on later in the morning. While they do that, I put the morning's arithmetic up on the board for them. Group 1 started ratios today and they haven't finished that so they can carry on where they left off. Group 2 are ready to start 'division of decimals'. I'll have to have them out at the board and go over it with them. The other group are still on 'money problems'. Gary was having trouble today but I think they'll be O.K. Paul and Martin have their own books to work from, but I'll have to spend some time with them to make sure they're getting on with it. Now, that will take us up to break. If any of them finish early, there are some cuboids we never finished making last week and they could carry on with those.
> After break, Paul and Martin go to Mrs S. for reading. It's our turn for the SRA box after break so we have to fit that in. Then at 11.30 we have a television programme – child labour in Victorian times, this week.
> In the afternoon, we'll probably talk about the programme and do some writing. There's a good story in their reading books about chimney sweeps – I think I'll use that to try and stimulate some writing. They'll be interested in the story – it's quite funny – especially after the television programme. I might get some good writing from them with that.
> For the last half hour, we have the gym. Mind you if it's like today, we'll probably play rounders on the field.

Although there may be certain merits in objectives-oriented planning, as mentioned earlier, teachers' 'natural' problem-solving approach could well be better suited to the normal classroom environment. To decide upon aims and objectives first may be quite unproductive when the final activity depends so much on a whole variety of more influential factors. There may well be occasions when thinking about objectives and the general purposes of the curriculum help to provide direction for teachers' planning efforts, but it may have limited value in teachers' everyday lesson planning.

Teachers' planning, of course, includes more than simply lesson preparation. It also involves making longer-term decisions about the curriculum. Yinger (1980), for example, distinguishes five levels of planning – yearly, termly, weekly, daily and lesson – and suggests that each is characterised by slightly different types of decisions, although those made at a higher level provide a framework for decisions made at lower levels. Longer term decisions tend to focus on general organisation whereas short-term planning decisions are concerned more with specific subject matter and activities. Whatever the level, however, teachers' planning appears to follow the problem-solving, as opposed to rational planning, approach.

The nature of teachers' long-term planning is illustrated in a case study of one primary school teacher at the start of a new school year (Clark and Elmore 1981). It was found that the teacher drew upon her knowledge of pupils, the available materials, and her previous experiences to plan out the year's work in general. Most of the decisions made consisted of which topics to include or omit, how best to sequence the topics and what materials might have to be made or ordered. The extent of her planning differed, however, for different subjects. The teacher was found to draw up quite a detailed schedule for mathematics, which she regarded as the most important area of the curriculum, and in this each term's work was mapped out in advance. In writing and in science, which she regarded as less structured and less important subject areas, far less detailed outlines were devised.

Interestingly, in McCutcheon's study of primary school teachers over the course of a year, it was found that they engaged in very little long-term planning. This was generally entrusted to the textbooks in use. A textbook would commonly be regarded as the year's work in that area of the curriculum. Several teachers in fact made more long-term decisions, concerning how pupils' progress through the book should be paced, towards the end of the year rather than the beginning, for it was then that they became concerned about finishing the book on time! McCutcheon's teachers generally did not favour long-term planning. They felt it was impossible to predict how pupils would progress or what interruptions might occur and that when long-term plans were made they frequently had to be drastically revised. The teachers were also aware of the constraining effects of long-term plans and the danger of becoming slaves to the plan, of being inflexible in their teaching and missing the unexpected learning opportunities that arose from time to time. Planning far ahead was regarded by most of the teachers as generally being an inefficient and unconstructive use of time.

Secondary school teachers' planning of new courses was studied by Taylor (1970). He investigated the process of course design and development in English, geography and science departments. Taylor took note of teachers' discussions about the courses, interviewed the teachers individually and undertook a questionnaire study of a larger sample. He similarly found that teachers' main considerations in planning were subject matter and the pupils. Rather than starting with an idea of the objectives they wished to achieve, the teachers' thoughts and discussions centred on what was possible, given the materials available and the pupils in the school, and it was from these considerations that a syllabus eventually emerged.

Planning, it would seem, at whatever level, involves a much greater consideration of the teaching context and a lesser concern with objectives than planning theorists have imagined.

THE EFFECTS OF PLANNING

As suggested earlier, teachers may engage in different types of lesson planning on different occasions. The nature of their planning may be determined by a variety of factors such as the subject matter involved, the teachers' familiarity with that area of the curriculum, and characteristics of the class. The planning of an arithmetic lesson, for example, may involve referring to the next exercise in the textbook, considering its suitability for the class, and deciding what explanations or instructions may be required before the children can tackle it, and perhaps whether any additional exercises or other resources will be needed (e.g. for the more able or less able children in the class). In areas of the curriculum which are not so strictly sequenced and are less tied to textbooks, such as social studies, science in the primary school or English in the secondary school, planning could be quite different and would probably require teachers to rely much more upon their knowledge of pupils and subject matter to construct appropriate activities. Similarly, if a teacher is very familiar with the subject matter and pupils to be taught, planning may be much more routine than when teachers are faced with the task of teaching an unfamiliar class subject matter, which they will first have to learn themselves. Whether the class has a wide ability range and whether this necessitates group activities, and the nature of the activities themselves (discussion, group work, or individual work, for instance) can also determine the type of planning required.

Because different activities, subject matter and pupils may demand several types of preparation, it is impossible to identify one preferred or effective mode of planning. It would seem that the skills of planning lie not so much in the mastery of one technique but in knowing which technique suits the occasion.

Nevertheless, teachers have been found to adopt certain preferred styles of planning. Clark and Yinger (1980) for example, comment on two planning styles which they have observed in teachers, namely *incremental planning* and *comprehensive planning*. Incremental planning involves little thought in advance about the lesson or its wider curricular context, and the teacher seems more intent upon trying ideas out in practice before moving on to the next stage of planning. Comprehensive planning, on the other hand, involves more thought both about individual lessons and about their place within the whole course. Clark and Yinger suggest that incremental planners put a high value on spontaneity, of staying in close contact with their pupils' interests and on the day-to-day development of their knowledge and skills.

Comprehensive planners have a clearer idea of the knowledge and skills they wish to achieve. However, Clark and Yinger found that although teachers may have a preferred style, they did change their style on some occasions. In particular, where teachers were familiar with the activities to be planned and could confidently estimate the pupils' reactions to them, they were more likely to use a comprehensive planning style. Incremental planning was much more likely to be in evidence when teachers encountered unfamiliar activities or pupils.

Certainly, there do appear to be some fairly consistent differences among teachers in their approaches to planning. Some teachers, for example, do a lot of systematic lesson planning. Others appear to rely very much on classroom routine, and their planning is mostly done in odd moments during teaching when they snatch time to think about what comes next. However, this type of 'survival planning' is not to be recommended. It inevitably adds to the burden of things that teachers have to think about during lessons, and possibly increases the stress that some teachers already experience. Entering the classroom with a well-thought-out plan probably provides most teachers with greater confidence and leads to a more relaxed lesson.

Some individual differences in planning were noted in a study by Peterson, Marx and Clark (1978), in which twelve teachers were provided with a package of materials concerning a town in France and a list of social studies objectives. They were given 90 minutes in which to plan three 50 minute lessons, providing a running commentary upon their thoughts as they did so. After planning the lessons, the teachers taught them to a group of eight pupils. This procedure was repeated on a further two occasions later in the same week. Peterson, Marx and Clark analysed teachers' commentaries in terms of the types of comments made, e.g. whether they concerned objectives, subject matter, the pupils, etc. The proportions of each of these comments was found to be fairly stable for each teacher but varied considerably between individuals. Furthermore, Peterson, Marx and Clark found some interesting correlations between certain types of planning and teachers' performance on tests of mental abilities. In particular, teachers who scored highly on a test of conceptual level, indicating an ability to differentiate problems highly, tended to consider the pupils and the instructional process more in their planning. Those with low conceptual level scores tended to focus more on lower-order subject matter. Such a finding probably has little practical application but the fact that abilities to conceptualise and solve problems are related to teachers' modes of planning lends some support to the notion that problem-solving occupies a central role in the planning process.

Relatively few studies have explored the effects of different types of planning, and these have tended to leave out of account the complicating effects of different teaching or subject matter contexts. Nevertheless, some interesting general conclusions have emerged.

Some types of planning have been found to be positively counter-productive in terms of pupil achievement. In order to promote learning, teachers must be able to assess pupils' competence and performance and match the learning experiences to suit the children. Yet some plans appear to act in such a way as to prevent teachers tuning in to cues about pupils' knowledge and understanding, and consequently impede class-room learning.

Zahorik (1970), for example, conducted an experiment in which six teachers were given plans which provided detailed objectives for a lesson on credit cards, a topic chosen for its lack of familiarity to teachers in their normal curriculum. The teachers were asked to examine and modify the plans to suit their own situation or preferred style of teaching and then to teach the lesson to their own class of ten-year-olds. Another six teachers with classes of the same age and in similar schools were asked to reserve 30 minutes of the school day for an experiment. Immediately before this period they were asked to teach a lesson on credit cards. All the lessons were tape-recorded and an analysis of the teacher–pupil interactions revealed some significant differences between the two groups. In particular, those teachers with detailed lesson objectives were less responsive to pupils' own ideas, whereas the teachers without plans were more receptive to pupils' ideas and more often developed them in discussion. We must be careful, however, in interpreting the significance of this finding. The lack of any plan at all may well have 'forced' one group of teachers to rely more on suggestions from the pupils to keep the lesson going, and in reality of course there are occasions when it is desirable not to respond to pupils' ideas and suggestions. Nevertheless, it is of interest that the teachers with detailed plans behaved quite differently in the classroom from those without.

A similar constraining effect of planning was found in the Peterson, Marx and Clark study described above. Teachers planned lessons using the same materials on three occasions during the week and on each occasion taught the lesson to a different but comparable group of pupils. At the end of each lesson the pupils' knowledge and understanding of the material was assessed by means of a multiple-choice test and an essay test. The researchers had expected that increased opportunity to plan and increased familiarity with the materials would lead to improved teacher effectiveness. In fact, the opposite occurred. Over the three occasions, eight of the teachers became steadily less effective. Four teachers who were not very effective on the first occasion improved on the second, but decreased on the third. A number of alternative explanations could account for these trends. Possibly the teachers became bored with the experiment and their lack of enthusiasm led to low levels of pupil attention and consequent poor performance on the tests. The explanation favoured by the researchers, however, is that overplanning, and in particular, too great an emphasis on mapping out the subject matter, led the teachers to pay little attention to the pupils' responses to the material. To illustrate, probably every teacher has experienced at least one occasion when a lesson which was well received by one class is remembered and used with another. The lesson is implemented exactly as before but the children respond with little enthusiasm, and appear to learn little. The memory of how the lesson went previously sometimes leads to inflexibility where the teacher fails to take account of the different children, their different interests and understanding and fails to respond to their reactions during the course of the lesson. A similar effect is often evident in students' preparation and response to examinations. If students have anticipated the questions, revised well and carefully prepared and memorised their set answers, these will tend to be written down in the examination whether they suit the question or not!

This inflexibility which appears to result from rigid planning, or too great a concern with communicating subject matter and insufficient concern with monitoring pupils, is often also evident in the first two or three lessons of student teachers. Typically, novice teachers, lacking confidence, plan by writing down the very words they intend to speak and the actions they intend to carry out, even noting when they will write on the blackboard. When delivering the lesson, these notes are simply read out. The students' anxiety in the situation, coupled with a total concern with implementing the plan, often prevents them from attending to cues concerning whether or not children are paying attention or whether or not they have understood. Consequently, student teachers' very first attempts at class teaching are often characterised by a distinct detachment from the rest of classroom life.

In another study of teacher planning and its effects, Morine (1976) selected a sample of twenty primary teachers who demonstrated instructional effectiveness in an experimental learning situation and compared their planning with another group of twenty teachers, whose effectiveness was judged to be low on the same criteria. The teachers were asked to write down their plans for the lessons taught to their normal classes. In comparing these plans it was found that the effective teachers, particularly those of younger children, took much greater account of pupils' abilities. They planned activities for a larger number of groups and sometimes even for individual children. The effective teachers of younger children referred much more to specific pupil competencies and difficulties (e.g. whether the children recognised the 'ch' blend). The instructionally effective teachers appeared to be much more oriented towards learning and considerate of the difficulties of individual pupils in their planning.

Teachers' knowledge of pupils would seem to be important both in terms of designing activities which are appropriate for particular groups, classes or individuals, and also in terms of monitoring or adjusting the activity in the classroom to ensure that the pupils learn from it. In monitoring activities, for example, teachers must be able to identify when certain facial expressions, work rates or noise from particular pupils signal difficulty or lost interest. In a later study, Morine investigated the planning of a group of teachers, their assessments of the pupils in the class and also teachers' stimulated recall commentaries (Morine-Dershimer 1979) and suggested that when lessons do not appear to be going as planned, teachers start to think more about their pupils (e.g. why are they not interested? or why have they misunderstood?). In all but the most inappropriate lessons, however, the teachers were found to have a routine response for correcting these situations and bringing the lesson back near its intended course.

We can at present conclude little about the effects of alternative planning styles. We know that planning is influential in determining classroom managerial and instructional processes, but different teachers faced with different contexts, pupils and materials and designing a variety of activities may find they have to plan in alternative ways. We do know however, that planning, as it occurs in everyday teaching, is a problem-solving process which can be demanding in terms of time and effort, and a number of suggestions can be made for improving the level of institutional support for teacher planning.

At present, planning is a rather neglected, undervalued aspect of teachers' work. Although much of the thinking that guides classroom activities occurs during lesson planning, teachers receive little official time or assistance for this. Planning is generally an individual pursuit involving minimal consultation with others. Yet if the opportunities and encouragement were provided for teachers to discuss with others their experiences on planning, it might be found that teachers have valuable knowledge to exchange.

McCutcheon suggests that school administrators can contribute a great deal to improving the quality of planning in schools, not only by helping to provide time and support, but by reducing the level of classroom interruptions which she suggests negate the effects of planning. It is argued that the many minor interruptions that occur during the course of class teaching – visitors, administrative queries, notification of timetable changes – contribute to an environment in which teachers feel planning is a waste of time.

In addition, teachers themselves must become aware of the nature and effects of their planning and be alerted to the possibilities of their plans being rigid and inflexible and consequently leading to an insensitivity to the teaching-learning process. Plans for teaching, it would seem, might more appropriately act like maps, keeping teachers informed of the route but always leaving the option of occasional and necessary detours open. Flexibility may have to be 'planned'.

MANAGING THE CURRICULUM

The term *curriculum* has come to refer not only to the knowledge and skills that schools impart but also to the methods of teaching used in doing this. Decisions about what ought to be taught and how are value judgements which are made by people and agencies both within and beyond the school, and such decisions obviously influence how teachers plan and teach. The recommendations of HMIs, the curriculum guidelines of LEAs, externally set examinations and policy decisions within the school may all contribute to the syllabus that a teacher is expected to follow and the materials that are made available. In addition, colleagues, parents and others may have certain expectations which might be influential in determining the activities that a teacher plans for the classroom. Teachers themselves may also have strong ideas about the nature of the curriculum but these may have to be adjusted to suit the materials, syllabus and expectations of others in the school who hold some influence over what the teacher does. For example, a secondary school mathematics teacher recounted to the author how he used to teach chess to a low-ability class during maths periods. He sincerely believed that for pupils who could not cope with the normal curriculum, spending half their maths periods learning to play chess helped to develop skills in logical thinking which contributed to improved mathematical understanding. However, it was an argument that obviously did not persuade his head of department, headteacher or for that matter some of the parents, all of whom possessed quite different, more traditional conceptions of schoolwork. Together they made it quite clear that he would rapidly have to change his ideas.

One of the functions which planning fulfils is to translate curriculum ideas and provisions into schemes for action in the classroom. The process of implementation, however, is not straightforward. Over the past decade or two there have been enormous changes in curricular recommendations and provisions. Primary education, with a plethora of new maths curriculum packages, reading laboratories, science and in some cases even foreign language teaching, bears little resemblance to the primary education of the late 1950s or even early 1960s. In secondary education, the introduction of comprehensive schools and the demand for a secondary education which is more relevant to society's needs has led to considerable experimentation, such as integrated science classes, mixed-ability teaching, careers education, sex education, and computer studies. Most of the initiatives for innovation have developed outside the school, from the DES, local education authorities or from curriculum development agencies such as the now defunct Schools Council. The innovations are generally communicated to teachers in the form of written guidelines and recommendations, or in the form of teachers' handbooks to accompany particular curriculum materials. Many innovations, however, have not been successfully implemented within schools and frequently when new ideas are put into practice they often do not operate as they were initially intended (see Stenhouse 1975, Lawton 1980).

The process by which innovations are translated or fail to be translated into classroom practice has understandably attracted considerable attention. Why do teachers appear to be very inefficient mediators in putting the curriculum into action? What happens in teachers' planning and thinking about the curriculum that contributes to these results?

Research on teachers' responses to new curriculum materials, using questionnaires and interviews, suggests that teachers' prime concern in considering innovations is with the subject matter that is covered and whether the materials are appropriate and interesting for the children they teach. In contrast, teachers appear to express little interest in new curriculum objectives, or prescribed changes in teaching processes (Shipman 1974, Ben-Peretz and Tamir 1981).

Doyle and Ponder (1977) suggest that teachers approach curriculum innovations as *pragmatic sceptics*, investigating innovations with the intention of achieving practical, workable solutions to the problems and difficulties they face in the classroom. Teachers' decisions about whether, how and to what extent an innovation is incorporated into existing practice are, they suggest, made on the basis of the teachers' knowledge of what works in classrooms and what is possible. Teachers, they claim, make decisions about the curriculum in accordance with a *practicality ethic*, which Doyle and Ponder further analyse into three basic criteria. The first, *instrumentality*, refers to whether innovation can be immediately implemented in the classroom. An innovation that consists of abstract ideas or general principles which cannot be easily understood or demonstrated is less likely to be adopted than an innovation which is ready for teachers to use. The second, *congruence*, is the extent to which the innovation can be incorporated into the teachers' normal style of teaching and with the type of pupils and in the contexts in which they normally work. The third, *cost*, refers to the amount of time, effort and money that will have to be expended in order to implement the innovation in the classroom. A high cost does not necessarily imply that the innovation is unacceptable, but the benefits of the innovation in terms of pupil learning or interest, for example, will have to make the extra cost worth while.

Doyle and Ponder suggest that if an innovation is high in instrumentality and congruence and low on cost relative to the expected effects of the innovation, there is a greater chance of it being implemented in the classroom. This account may well explain the success or failure of certain curriculum innovations. For example, the notion of discovery learning has not been widely implemented in the secondary school science curriculum. Brown and McIntyre (1982) argue that it is not understood by teachers and does not fit their familiar practice, and is therefore either not implemented or implemented in ways that differ from the curriculum developers' expectations. Consequently, they suggest Doyle and Ponder's account provides quite an appropriate explanation for the failure of this innovation.

However, on some occasions teachers probably employ criteria other than those outlined by Doyle and Ponder. For example, in spite of an innovation having high practicality, teachers may regard it as experimental and unestablished and not in the best interests of their pupils to adopt at the present time. It is also not inconceivable that teachers' responses to innovation may on occasion be influenced by their own ideological beliefs. For example, if a science teacher strongly believes that the purpose of science teaching in schools is to equip pupils with the skills to solve scientific problems rather than encourage pupils to amass a knowledge of scientific facts, some textbooks and innovatory science materials would immediately be more appealing than others. In addition, decisions to adopt or adapt a new curriculum are often made by heads of departments or by a promoted member of staff and the decision may be made in the light of current popular beliefs about the teaching of that subject or current recommendations from the LEA or DES, and also practical considerations like the availability of finance.

Classroom teachers may not have much influence in determining the classroom materials with which they are provided and may therefore find themselves with an innovation that they are expected to implement. Teachers, however, have to cope with other constraints as well as the materials and curriculum guidelines with which they are presented. Teachers' planning, as earlier indicated, is a problem-solving process in which a number of factors have to be taken into account. Olson (1980), in carrying out case studies of three comprehensive schools which were implementing the Schools Council Integrated Science Project (SCISP), suggests that when presented with a new package of materials, teachers select from it those parts which appear to be most useful to them in their particular context. Olson draws an analogy between implementing a new curriculum and assembling an Airfix kit without the instructions: teachers select those parts that look as though they might fit and incorporate them into their familiar practice.

Frequently, the demands of a new curriculum will conflict with the demands of the teacher's classroom context. Olson, for example, suggests that in the traditional science classroom, filling up notebooks with notes and neat diagrams is a significant part of the work. Full, neat notebooks are a way of indicating to pupils and parents and also to themselves that both teacher and pupils have done their work. The quality and fullness of notebooks have become accepted criteria for judging the effectiveness of teaching. SCISP, however, involves more emphasis on discussion and experimentation and requires minimal note-taking, thus depriving teachers of this means of demonstrating their effectiveness. A common response to this dilemma observed by Olson, is to restructure the SCISP discussion notes, originally intended to stimulate class discussions, into notes to be copied into the notebooks, thereby satisfying the established criteria!

Hamilton (1975) provides further examples of such conflict, again in some case studies of integrated science teaching. He points out how various features of the school context, such as the low prestige given to teaching in the lower school where integrated science teaching is concentrated, and the maintenance of separate physics, chemistry and biology departments, and the few opportunities for professional discussions amongst the staff contribute to keeping integration at a superficial level.

A further example of the ineffective translation of curriculum ideas into practice is provided by the recent primary mathematics schemes. As outlined in Chapter 3, these assume that teachers possess a repertoire of group teaching and management skills that probably few teachers possess. Consequently, the schemes tend to operate in practice quite differently from how their designers intended, resulting in much instruction being done by the materials or the pupils themselves rather than by the teacher.

Although attempted innovation in the school curriculum is now commonplace, often little help is given to teachers to help them adjust to the demands of new materials or teaching approaches. Rarely do they have the opportunity to think out the full implications of the innovation for their classroom practice. In consequence, when teachers are faced with the task of coping with the immediate day-to-day events of the classroom it is not surprising that they implement the familiar plan or respond with the well-practised routine, rather than deciding upon actions which better suit the innovation. Many curriculum innovations consequently have superficial impact on classroom life.

IMPLICATIONS FOR MANAGING THE CURRICULUM

Curriculum innovation can be viewed as typically involving the change of parts of the framework within which teachers plan. New materials or new recommendations for practice, however, do not necessarily produce the expected changes in classroom processes. Teachers have to respond to the whole framework or context in which they find themselves and sometimes the demands of the innovation conflict with others.

Research into the processes of curriculum innovation and implementation have pointed out some of these difficulties in practice and the findings of such research suggest various recommendations for more effective control of the curriculum.

First, given that the initiative for innovation generally arises outside the school and that the nature of the innovation is often decided by people other than those ultimately responsible for its implementation, there is a strong case for the curriculum developer to appreciate more fully the context of the classroom teacher. Although many innovations include field trials and involve teachers in their development, the trials are generally brief and consultation with teachers is often upon content rather than issues concerning its adoption and use in the classroom. The problems that face the curriculum developer in producing an innovation are not the same problems facing classroom teachers. If curriculum developers could work more closely with teachers, appreciate the context in which the intended innovation will operate, and understand how teachers will translate the proposal into action, one would expect the chances of implementation to be much higher.

Second, it is clear that teachers themselves have important knowledge and experience to contribute to our understanding of the processes of innovation. Until recently, very few initiatives for change have emerged and developed within schools themselves. Teachers generally lack the time, financial and material aid, expert help and sometimes institutional support to undertake innovation on any large scale. Nevertheless, teachers are familiar with the context in which they work and the pupils they teach. They are in a position to judge what will work in schools and what will not, the effects that certain innovations may have and when other changes, such as training, facilities or class structures, are necessary in order to enable some innovations to succeed. Classroom teachers by coming to understand their own role in the translation of the curriculum into practice have a valuable contribution to make to future curricular developments.

Third, teachers need help and support in adjusting to innovations. Brown and McIntyre point out the important role of the assistant head of department in some Scottish schools which were found to cope more successfully with science innovation. Informal discussions about the curriculum, teaching methods and particular classroom problems were common between teachers and those assistant heads who were enthusiastic about the innovation, specific difficulties being discussed and sometimes quickly resolved. It is suggested that this type of informal and readily available support, as opposed to the more formal contacts with the head of department, has an important contribution to make in facilitating change.

Although there may be various opinions about the nature of changes that should occur in the school curriculum, there can be little doubt that changes are essential. However, if new ideas are to be successfully translated into action in the classroom, there is clearly a need for teachers, curriculum developers, and those in authority within schools, to come to a fuller understanding of the processes involved in planning and classroom teaching, and a need for greater co-operation among them.

RECOMMENDED READING

Barnes, D. (1982) *Practical Curriculum Study*. London: Routledge and Kegan Paul.
Intended for students in training, this guide reviews issues and problems concerning course planning and curriculum design. Considers different modes of planning and their appropriateness in different contexts. Provides numerous practical exercises.
Lawton, D. (1980) *The Politics of the School Curriculum*. London: Routledge and Kegan Paul.
Examines the question of where control of the curriculum in English schools lies, traces the origins of the movement for greater teacher accountability, and considers reforms that might facilitate the control and innovation of education.
McCutcheon, G. (1980) 'How do elementary school teachers plan? The nature of planning and influences on it'. *The Elementary School Journal* **81**(1), pp. 4–23.
A very readable investigation of the planning of 24 US primary school teachers, conducted over the course of a year.
Stenhouse, L. (1975) *An Introduction to Curriculum Research and Development*. London: Heinemann.
An easily followed account of the development of alternative models of the curriculum and of teachers' involvement in this innovation.

EXERCISES

1. Plan a lesson on a specific topic for a class with which you are familiar. State what you wish the pupils to do, and indicate how your time and theirs would be occupied during the lesson. What assumptions have you made about the

pupils, their previous learning experiences and about the materials and classroom context? What managerial and instructional problems might you encounter in such a lesson with this class?

2. Consider how each of the following factors might influence your planning of the above lesson: a class with a wide ability range; an unfamiliar class; a shortage of materials; your lesson timetabled for last period on a Friday.

3. Taking one subject area at a particular level (e.g. mathematics for first year juniors) consider the long-term planning decisions that you would make and the help that you would seek in making them (a) before the start of the year, (b) early in the year after you have become familiar with the pupils in the class. How would you justify this approach to long-term planning?

4. Looking at one text or curriculum package, outline the assumptions that appear to have been made about the context in which it will be used and the nature of teaching/learning processes. Does it demand any rare or special skills of teachers? How would you decide upon its suitability for a class and school with which you are familiar?

5

The Context of Teaching

TEACHERS are commonly believed to possess a high level of professional autonomy. Equally, they are often held responsible, either collectively or individually, for the events in their classrooms and for the effects of their teaching. When dissatisfaction is expressed with education – claims of falling standards of attainment or poor classroom behaviour – it is frequently teachers who become a ready target for blame. But how autonomous are teachers? How much freedom do they really have in deciding the affairs of their classroom? For what can teachers reasonably be held responsible?

There are certainly areas where individual teachers appear to have very little freedom to determine classroom events. Their practice is often constrained in numerous and quite complex ways. Consider, for example, an LEA which adopts particular tests to monitor pupil performance in certain subject areas. Teachers inevitably feel under some pressure to emphasise the test-related topics in the curriculum to ensure that their class or their school performs favourably. The tests therefore come to influence what is taught within the schools. Lawton (1980) in fact suggests that the decision to establish the Assessment of Performance Unit to monitor standards of attainment nationally was premised on such an assumption. He argues that by introducing the regular monitoring of certain subject areas, the DES has, by subtle means, increased central control of the curriculum and reduced teacher autonomy.

The prevalence of note-taking activities in some secondary schools might be similarly attributed to certain influences and constraints, including an external examination system and a form of accountability that has developed in some schools whereby teachers' status or professional worth is largely assessed in terms of their pupils' examination passes. The pressure to achieve a high success rate coupled with a common belief that a good set of notes is the key to examination success can lead to a rather dull programme of teaching and learning.

Particular actions in the classroom may also be partly the product of certain influences and constraints. On occasions teachers may find themselves engaged in an interesting discussion with pupils, for example, but feel obliged to change the topic or the activity because it does not relate to the syllabus, or because they think parents, the headteacher or colleagues would disapprove of class time being used in this way.

Establishing behavioural norms in the classroom is another area of practice which can be strongly influenced by the context in which teachers work. Trying to achieve quietness in the classroom, for example, is exceptionally difficult when the pupils are aware that other teachers in the school tolerate classroom noise. Similarly, entire schools may find it difficult to maintain certain standards of behaviour if these are not valued or supported in the local community.

Teachers are also expected to conform to various school policies and practices which might frequently reflect external influences and constraints and be at odds with their own preferred practice. The keeping of neat workbooks and a policy of always correcting spellings, punctuation and grammar, for example, may in some cases owe as much to parental pressure and demands to keep up appearances as to any beliefs about appropriate instruction, children's learning or the development of desirable work habits.

It is clearly not difficult to think of a wide range of examples where teachers' behaviour appears to be shaped by a variety of factors. In some cases, the influences and constraints upon teachers are quite remote from their immediate environment (e.g. DES policy) but they nonetheless appear to filter down through various agencies and individuals, eventually to affect what teachers do in the classroom. Teachers themselves may well have a set of personal beliefs about the nature of teaching and how they should carry out their work, but, in the process of translating these into action, other factors frequently seem to have a powerful effect upon the outcome.

If teachers' practice is indeed at least partly determined by the context in which they work, it is obviously important for teachers, curriculum designers, educational administrators and others concerned with teaching and learning to discover the significant features of this context and the process by which their influence is exerted, so that attempts to improve the quality of classroom life are more constructive.

What then are the influences and constraints upon teachers? How do they relate to teachers' practice?

TEACHERS' PERCEIVED INFLUENCES AND CONSTRAINTS

One obvious approach to identifying the influences and constraints upon teachers is to ask them. The first investigation to pursue this line of enquiry was Taylor's (1974) study of primary school teachers. He first of all collected several teachers' reports of the influences and constraints they experienced in daily teaching. He defined *influences* in terms of those people or agencies which helped teachers to achieve their aims, whereas *constraints* were defined in terms of those factors which prevented them. A questionnaire was then constructed which represented the range of teachers' reported influences and constraints. This was presented to teachers in twelve schools who were asked to rate each influence on a 1 to 5 scale according to (a) the extent it influenced affairs within the *school* and (b) the extent it influenced affairs within the *classroom*; to indicate whether they felt they could reciprocate each influence (i.e. exert some control over it); and to check those constraints they felt prevented them from achieving their aims. The same teachers had also previously completed a questionnaire enquiring about their teaching aims.

Taylor's study is a survey of teachers' perceived influences and constraints. It assumes that some factors are generally 'influencing' whereas others are generally 'constraining'. In reality, this is probably not the case. One factor may act as influence or constraint with different teachers in different contexts. The same factor may even act as influence and constraint at the same time. A syllabus, for example, may restrict what teachers can do and therefore be a constraint, but may at the same time aid teachers by reducing the demand for detailed planning and therefore also be an influence. Nevertheless, Taylor's study does provide us with some interesting and valuable insight into teachers' perceptions, indicating those factors that teachers perceive as being generally helpful or unhelpful in carrying out their work.

In examining reported influences at the school level, Taylor found that teachers rated the headteacher as the strongest influence, followed by colleagues, pupils, deputy head, the formal staff meeting and the informal staff group. The teachers clearly perceived their schools as having a fairly authoritarian system of control. Apart from the headteacher, and to a lesser extent the deputy head, power to influence school affairs was only attributed to the collective efforts of individuals or 'pressure groups'. Interestingly, the pupils were rated as marginally more influential than the formal staff meeting; and both colleagues and pupils were rated as more influential than the deputy head. HMIs, LEA advisors, parents, local colleges and universities and even the teachers themselves were not perceived as influential at all. Teachers' impressions of school control suggest an image of schools being under the relatively independent authority of the headteacher.

At the classroom level, however, teachers' perceptions of influences were rather different. Teachers perceived themselves to be by far the greatest influence upon what happened in their classrooms, with the pupils, headteacher, colleagues and informal staff group exerting some influence. Again, parents, HMIs, LEA advisors, and local colleges and universities were rated as having little influence. The teachers obviously felt quite autonomous in deciding classroom affairs and reported being influenced only by those personnel most immediately involved in their day-to-day classroom life. This finding is also supported by the fact that teachers within the same school were found to possess widely different educational aims, thus not appearing to conform to any one view. Teachers, it would seem, tend to confirm the opinion that once the classroom door is closed it is they who are in command.

Of the 28 listed influences upon school and classroom affairs, parents were the only influence which a substantial number of teachers felt they could reciprocate. 42 per cent of the teachers thought they could exert some control over the influence of parents. Other influences were perceived by a large majority to be beyond individual teachers' control.

The most common areas of perceived constraint concerned the immediate classroom environment. The number of children in the class, the children's home environment, and the size of classrooms were the most frequently mentioned. The provision of teaching materials, ancillary help and storage space were also fairly commonly perceived sources of constraint. It would seem to be fairly well agreed among the teachers that the constraints are mostly in the personnel and materials with which they have to work.

Further support for Taylor's findings concerning teachers' views of their own influence in the school and in the classroom comes from a study of Scottish primary teachers. Hobbs, Kleinberg and Martin (1979) investigated teachers' and headteachers' views of who ought to make the decisions regarding the organisation and administration of the mathematics and art curricula, and of how such decisions were in fact made within the school. In general, it was found that teachers felt they should be responsible for class-related decisions such as deciding the frequency of homework or the amount of class time that would be devoted to maths, and felt they should be consulted by the head and promoted staff when it came to major decisions such as choosing the school maths scheme or the type of progress records to be kept. The majority of heads, on the other hand, felt they ought to be in command. They wished to be involved in most decisions and solely responsible for major curricular and organisational ones.

It is interesting that teachers' and headteachers' accounts of how decisions were in fact made within the school varied considerably even within the same schools. In general, however, headteachers reported being in control of administrative and organisational decisions whereas teachers typically reported having less influence than they would like. Teachers, it would seem, regard headteachers as exercising considerable influence in matters of school policy and at least some influence in matters of classroom practice.

UNPERCEIVED INFLUENCES AND CONSTRAINTS

Not all influences and constraints upon teachers' practice, however, are perceived by teachers. For example, the influence of HMIs upon what is taught in the classroom is regarded by teachers in Taylor's study as very weak. Yet HMI policy documents may well be influential in shaping the views of LEA advisors and administrators whose views in turn may influence headteachers to adapt school policy or curriculum guidelines, eventually influencing teachers' practice. Moreover, school visits by HMIs, which result in written reports upon the school may also result in changes in school organisation, and school policy regarding teaching methods or curriculum content. These indirect influences upon teachers' practice may perhaps go unnoticed by teachers themselves.

In addition, some influences and constraints may only be evident on rare occasions. Hobbs, Kleinberg and Martin suggest that the low level of consensus within schools concerning who makes particular decisions may be explained in terms of the common ambiguity surrounding school decision-making. Teachers may believe themselves to be responsible for certain decisions and might only discover otherwise if their consequent actions conflict with the intentions of the head. As long as headteachers' preferences and teachers' actions are in accord, both may believe themselves to be in control! It may in fact only be in such situations as staff meetings to discuss school policy or in confrontations with the head, parents or inspectors that teachers may come to question their actual autonomy in certain areas.

The William Tyndale School provided a classic example of a sudden confrontation with constraints (see Gretton and Jackson 1975). This junior school in the London borough of Islington achieved notoriety in the mid-1970s when the head and some of its staff decided to make radical changes in the curriculum and introduce what was regarded by others as a *laissez-faire* style of leadership. The teachers believed themselves to be exercising their professional rights to decide what happened within their own institution, and in any event considered themselves to be working within the broad guidelines of the LEA in its proposal for more democratically run schools. However, outraged parents who complained of chaotic, unproductive activities received considerable support from the press and brought pressure to bear upon the LEA, which was legally responsible for the running of the school. The school was eventually closed and the 'rebel' teachers dismissed. Although parents are not assigned a powerful role in the control of our education system, the William Tyndale affair indicates how power can sometimes be wielded unofficially, particularly when individuals resort to collective action.

Another type of influence or constraint upon teachers are the common beliefs or ideologies held by the staff of a school. It has been argued that schools possess an ethos (e.g. Sharp and Green 1975), a set of jointly held beliefs, traditions and taken-for-granted practices. Teachers within the same school, though they may differ somewhat in their views on education and also in their classroom practices, do, it is suggested, share and support a common core of beliefs about pupils, teachers and teaching.

The influence of these beliefs is perhaps most noticeable to teachers at the start of their career when they first confront the task of adjusting to life within the school. This is well illustrated in a series of case studies by Hanson and Herrington (1976) who followed student primary teachers through their final year of training and their first year of employment in schools. They found that beginning teachers commonly reported problems of adjustment to the school, and initial difficulties in adopting the 'normal' teacher role. As students and later as probationer teachers, they were aware of the expectations of the head and other staff in the school that they adopt an authoritarian role in the classroom, a role in which many of the beginning teachers experienced considerable discomfort. The pupil behaviours which teachers clamped down on, like the tapping of feet or ensuring that the teacher was correctly addressed when spoken to, seemed at first petty and unimportant. Yet, by deliberately correcting pupils at fault in front of beginning teachers, heads and other teachers communicated the expectations for teacher conduct. After a few weeks, the beginning teachers in fact found themselves chastising pupils for the same behaviours, having gradually come to accept the authoritarian role.

Several studies of teachers' attitudes before, during and after training have demonstrated some dramatic shifts in attitude in different phases of their career (see Morrison and McIntyre 1973, Tabachnick et al.

1982). Before training, teachers appear to have quite traditional, authoritarian views about teaching and the role of the teacher. During training, students become more liberal, 'progressive' and child-centred in orientation, yet this quickly reverses towards the end of the training period, and once teachers are employed in the classroom, they appear to regain strong beliefs about teacher authority and the control of pupils.

It has often been argued that schools have a powerful 'wash-out' effect upon teacher training (Zeichner and Tabachnick 1981). While teacher training institutions may attempt to encourage more liberal attitudes and new practices in their students, the school institution exerts a powerful influence upon its new teachers which cancels out the effects of such training, and encourages latent views about teaching, first formulated whilst a pupil, to emerge and become supported. Hanson and Herrington's case studies certainly suggest that most beginning teachers fairly quickly come to share the traditional beliefs and practices of the school. One of their teachers did attempt to resist the pressure to change her views and practices, and persisted in implementing a system of classroom organisation and a social climate that differed from the norm. Pupils, for instance, were allowed to follow their own interests as long as they completed the daily work quota. The head, however, disapproved. After frequent warnings, 'kindly tolerance and advice' changed to 'explicit, authoritarian control'. The teacher was eventually relieved of her class and made a 'floating teacher', a capacity in which she moved around other classes giving lessons which were already planned and tightly structured for her. Even though she had been awarded high grades on student teaching practice, she was informed by her headteacher that she would not pass her probationary year. Her appeals to the LEA and her teacher union enlisted no support.

Hanson and Herrington present the process of transition into the role of teacher as a rather oppressive one in which the headteacher acts as a powerful mediator of an accepted set of beliefs and practices to which the beginning teacher has no alternative but conformity. However, other studies have suggested that the process of adjusting to the institutional life of the school is more complex.

Lacey (1977) proposes that new teachers play a far more active role in their adjustment to the school and describes three different types of response that they make to school constraints. *Internalised adjustment* occurs when teachers comply with accepted definitions and practices and believe that these are for the best. Teachers adapt their behaviour and also change their beliefs about good teaching. For example, they may come to accept that insisting upon silence in the classroom is essential for effective management, even though they had previously assumed that pupils talking in the classroom was simply a minor irritation. *Strategic compliance* occurs when teachers comply with traditional practices but do so in order to gain acceptance within the school or at least to avoid undesirable reactions. However, they maintain their own beliefs about teaching and are aware of the mismatch between their beliefs and the practices to which they feel obliged to conform. For example, what may appear to be petty school rules, such as having the children line up outside the classroom door before admitting them to the room, may be conformed to but still regarded as trivial. In *strategic redefinition*, teachers actually bring about change in the accepted practices of the school. Lacey claims that individual teachers are not in a dominant position within the organisation of the school, but can on occasions exercise influence over its commonly held beliefs and practices.

The case studies carried out by Lacey and also by Tabachnick et al. (1982) both tend to confirm that adjustment to institutional life is a rather complex negotiation in which the ideological constraints of the institution and teachers' own beliefs interact and both are changed in consequence. The extent to which the ideology of the school and the ideology of the individual teacher is affected seems to vary considerably from school to school and from individual to individual. Some teachers, perhaps as a result of their ability to negotiate personal relationships, their confidence in their own practice and their ability to defend it in discussion, or to resist criticism, appear to be largely unaffected by school pressures. It is not uncommon, for example, to find at least one or two teachers in a school who seem to have negotiated an independence which has come to be accepted by the rest of the staff, and who have become quite impervious to any influences irrespective of their source. Others have negotiated an independence but at some personal cost, such as loss of friendship or loss of personal influence with others.

Both Lacey and Tabachnick suggest that there are certain skills associated with adapting to institutional life and that teachers must learn to identify the constraints that might influence their practice and discover whether and how these influences can be negotiated: becoming a teacher involves becoming a functioning member of an institution. Unfortunately, little research has been carried out on the institutional adaptations of teachers and consideration of what these skills might be is largely speculative.

It has frequently been suggested that some educational ideologies are taken for granted by many teachers who remain largely unaware of their sometimes powerful effects. Sharp and Green (1975) for example, in a case study of a London infant school, indicate how a 'progressive' ideology and a set of beliefs which teachers had about their children could serve to obstruct the education of pupils from lower working-class families. Teachers believed that children who came from supportive homes (ones judged to be 'normal' by their own middle-class values) came to school with an interest in learning. Such children might be familiar with books, for example, express enthusiasm about learning, and be well-disposed to establishing an appropriate relationship with the teacher. These pupils were regarded as 'well-prepared' and 'ready to learn' and teachers provided them with useful learning activities. Children from lower working-class families, however, were typically regarded as 'deprived' or even 'maladjusted'. Teachers experienced difficulty in establishing a relationship with them, and reckoned that such pupils had missed out on essential pre-school activities and were not well-oriented towards learning. Consequently, children from lower working-class homes were left to play, and to 'develop' in their own time. Believing readiness to be an important pre-requisite for learning, coupled with certain beliefs about the children and the effects of their home background, resulted in children from more supportive or middle-class families receiving a lot of teachers' time and help and being encouraged to achieve, and lower working-class pupils generally receiving little.

However, there are other studies of teachers' classroom interaction that suggest teachers often spend more time instructing the less able in the class than they do the most able (see Brophy and Good 1974). Nevertheless, Sharp and Green's study does alert us to the possible effects of some popular educational beliefs, effects that may well be unnoticed by teachers themselves.

It has been similarly argued that other taken-for-granted assumptions about pupils concerning, for example, girls' lack of achievement in science and maths, or the attitudes and educational attainments of ethnic minority groups, can lead teachers to act differently towards certain groups of pupils in the classroom and thereby influence the pupils' attitudes and achievements (e.g. Rist 1970, Deem 1978). Such studies have attracted the attention of many sociologists of education, who have suggested that some teacher ideologies persist because they enable schools to serve a stratification function within society, maintaining the social divisions which currently exist (e.g. Lacey 1970, Woods 1979, Ball 1981). Ideology, it is argued, provides a rationale for schools to allocate their resources differentially, resulting in the most privileged groups within society receiving a better education, eventually receiving superior educational qualifications and therefore obtaining access to the more prestigious occupations and maintaining their privileged status.

Establishing associations between teacher ideologies, classroom practice and their effects is a somewhat speculative process, however. It is difficult to confirm whether particular beliefs of teachers do lead to particular practices, resulting in the claimed effects. Nevertheless, such studies may serve a 'sensitising' function (Elliott 1980, McCutcheon 1981) encouraging teachers and others to reflect upon their values and beliefs and consider their impact upon the nature of teaching and its consequences. The possibility that certain commonly held teaching ideologies have undesirable social effects certainly deserves careful consideration.

COPING STRATEGIES – RESPONSES TO CONSTRAINTS

It has often been suggested that some strategies are fairly common among teachers because they encounter similar constraints which shape their classroom practice. Lundgren (1974) for example, identified a common strategy adopted by a sample of Swedish mathematics teachers to cope with the problems presented by the range of abilities in class teaching. He hypothesised the notion of a *steering group*, a small group of pupils between the 10th and 25th percentiles of ability and found that their work rate was a good predictor of the rate at which teachers moved through the syllabus. Lundgren argues that, given classes with pupils of various abilities, it is difficult for teachers to know when it is appropriate to move on to the next topic. Rather than carefully monitor the performance of each individual pupil, he suggests teachers pay particular attention to the performance of the steering group. When the steering group have mastered a unit of the curriculum, it signals to the teacher that it is time to move on.

The realisation that teachers may well have developed a range of strategies for coping with the constraints of the classroom led Abrahamson and Westbury to coin the term *coping strategy* (see Westbury 1980). They argued that the recitation – a pattern of interaction in which teacher and pupils engage in fairly rapid question and answer exchanges – was one example of a coping strategy. Its widespread use in primary and secondary schools over the past fifty years was suggested to be due not to its effectiveness as an instructional technique, but to the common, unchanged constraints experienced by teachers in classrooms. Having 30 or so pupils to keep busy and learning over an allotted time with certain prescribed materials and content, Abrahamson and Westbury suggest that the recitation provides a way of coping with these multiple constraints. This has been questioned, however, by Stodolsky et al. (1981) who found that recitations are used in a variety of lesson contexts and at times appear to serve some very useful instructional functions.

In observing 58 mathematics and social studies classes over a period of two years, Stodolsky collected a large amount of data concerning the lesson contexts in which recitations occurred and the behaviour of teacher and pupils during these periods. She suggests that in recitations, pupils can be very attentive and engaged in cognitively demanding activities. She also points out five instructional functions that the recitation commonly serves: *reviewing* past learning at the beginning of a lesson or a new activity; *introducing new material* in an interactive manner, asking for pupil suggestions, ideas or comments as new information, skills or concepts are brought in; *checking answers to work* as in the case of marking homework or completed exercises and providing feedback; *practice* of new techniques; and *checking children's understanding of materials and ideas* to discover if they have acquired the appropriate knowledge and understanding.

Stodolsky suggests that in many cases, the recitation could be a very efficient and useful instructional process and warns of the dangers of assuming that the recitation is a response to constraints.

Attributing certain aspects of teachers' practice to the constraints in which they work is a very difficult and speculative task. Teachers may not themselves be aware, and therefore cannot give their accounts, of the constraints that affect their classroom behaviour. Alternatively, they may have been aware at one time of why a particular strategy developed but this may now have come to be an accepted, taken-for-granted aspect of their practice. In addition, teachers' behaviour is often the result of several motives and both distant and more proximal constraints which makes accounting for their behaviour all the more complex. Recitations can occur in various contexts and it is often difficult to identify reasons for why they take the form they do. In the following extract, for example, taken from a biology lesson in a public school, the recitation appears to be serving a function of controlling pupil behaviour and asserting teacher authority both through the teacher's frequent commands and his forms of address. It is also maintaining pupil attention with a brisk pace. There is a certain amount of humour, often at a pupil's expense, which may serve to relax the tension at times but possibly also helps to reinforce the authority and 'distance' of the teacher. However, in addition, the interactions are concerned with instruction, and the teacher is communicating the concept of irritability through analogies familiar to the children, though one might wish to question their appropriateness.

P. Sir it's stopped moving – I think it's dead.
T. So because it's stopped moving it's dead.
P. It's been, er, well, er...
T. Plants don't move do they?
P. It's been constantly moving all the time though, sir.
T. Boy, stop arguing. Now do plants move?
P. Well, er, sometimes, sir, well, er, not themselves.
T. Does an oak tree move – so it's dead?
P. Oh.
[*Laughter*]
T. No, you've observed something – it's stopped moving but it mightn't be dead. A lot of them may have stopped moving – I want you to try and think why that may have happened.
P. Because they're sensitive to light.
T. Because they're sensitive to light – perhaps – what else?
P. Chemicals ... heat.
T. Heat. Where's heat coming from?
P. From the light.
T. Yes in other words they may be showing ...
P. Irritability.
T. Irritability. What is irritability?
P. It's a response to outside stimuli.
T. It's a response to outside stimuli.
   [*T shouts*] Stand up. Look at me. Sit down. Shut up.
   [*Normal voice*] What's he just done?
P. Responded.
T. He's just shown irritability ... he's responded to the stimulus of my foot. What would you smell if you were walking round the market place on a Saturday night?
P. The fish and chip shop.
T. And where would you go if you had twenty pence in your pocket and hadn't eaten for three days?
P. The fish and chip shop.
T. You'd smell the fish and chip shop and head towards it – you're responding to outside stimuli. You're therefore exhibiting what?
P. Irritability.
Extract from Bliss (1976) 'Language use in contrasting schools'. Unpublished MEd thesis, University of Leicester. With kind permission.

Recitations may indeed enable teachers to cope with some of the constraints they encounter in everyday teaching but as Stodolsky points out, they may at the same time be quite efficient techniques for obtaining pupils' attention and instructing the class.

Woods (1979) discusses some of the difficulties in identifying the constraints upon teachers' practice. He argues that because teachers are often unaware of the constraints upon them or because they may not wish to admit to adopting certain coping strategies for reasons of self-esteem or professional image, and because the effects of constraints on classroom practice are not themselves easily observed, research on constraints must involve procedures which allow the researcher to develop insights into the usually hidden aspects of teaching. Woods adopted an *ethnographic* approach in his own study of a secondary school in the Midlands. He became a *participant observer*, taking part in the life of the school, helping teachers in classes and joining in staffroom conversation. His intention was 'to combine deep personal involvement and a measure of detachment' (p. 261). By observing and talking to teachers (and pupils), by coming to appreciate their motives and experiences, yet maintaining a detachment which enabled him to look at them critically, he aimed to develop an understanding of how the constraints upon teachers affected their classroom practice.

Woods suggests that the teachers in the school he studied were quite powerfully constrained, particularly by a shrinking supply of aid and resources and by pupils who were reluctant to learn and resentful of school. However, Woods points out that in the face of these constraints teachers felt a strong personal need to maintain a professional 'front', to present the impression that all was well in their classrooms and that they were coping satisfactorily. This resulted in many aspects of teachers' work having the appearance of teaching yet in fact being more concerned with coping with constraints. In particular, Woods identifies eight types of strategy which he calls *survival strategies*, that were commonly employed by teachers and which enabled them to cope within the classroom. These include *socialisation* in which teachers encourage pupils to conform to certain standards of dress and behaviour, such as how to walk in the corridors. These standards have little, if anything, to do with the business of education, but Woods argues that teachers invest considerable time in insisting on such standards in the belief that they encourage conformity in other areas and in particular dissuade pupils from disruption in the classroom. *Domination* is a strategy which relies on physical aggression or the threat of such aggression. Even when corporal punishment has been abolished, Woods argues that 'there is still a great deal of punching, knuckling, tweaking, clouting, slapping, slippering, hair-pulling, twisting, rulering and kicking' (p. 150), and suggests that many teachers rely on such techniques for maintaining classroom order. *Negotiation* refers to the trades and exchanges that teachers engage in to obtain conformity – for example, promises of a television programme or a film in exchange for doing some work. Some teachers adopted *fraternisation* strategies, attempting to reduce the conflict between teacher and pupils that arises from the professional demands upon teachers and the reluctance of pupils to be in school, by becoming 'one of the lads'. Exchanging dirty jokes and adopting the language of the pupils are examples that Woods reports of teachers attempting to reduce conflict in this way. *Absence* or *removal* includes a variety of strategies for reducing the contact between pupils and teacher, ranging from promoted staff timetabling themselves out of the difficult classes, to frequent sick-leave or sending the most troublesome pupils out of the school on link courses at the technical college or on community service. Woods suggests that teachers also commonly expend efforts in maintaining *ritual* and *routine* which helps to make school life more predictable and manageable and therefore less stressful, as in the case of regularly dictating notes and employing memory drills. *Occupational therapy* refers to attempts to keep children busy, generally in simple repetitive tasks, while not actually learning anything, again reducing the classroom demands upon the teacher. Finally, *morale-boosting* strategies were used to justify other strategies. These referred to the attempts teachers made to convince themselves and one another that they were truly engaged in the business of education and were doing their job well. In staffroom conversation, for example, teachers might support one another's perceptions of the children as 'thick' and 'slow' to justify the repetitive, 'busyness' of their classrooms.

To anyone who is familiar with an urban comprehensive school there is considerable realism in the strategies that Woods describes. However, at times, Woods's interpretation of events seems extreme. He suggests, for example, that teaching in the sense of instruction has, in the type of school in which he observed, largely disappeared. Faced with powerful constraints, teachers have substituted *teaching* with *survival*, superficially disguised to appear as teaching. Certainly many secondary school teachers would probably not argue that reluctant learners and declining resources are sometimes powerful and highly demotivating constraints, but it may be that instruction is embedded within, as opposed to substituted by, those apparent survival strategies. On occasions, it may even be quite inappropriate to describe these strategies in terms of survival. They may sometimes be consciously and deliberately employed by teachers with the intention of aiding instruction or making school experience more rewarding for the pupils, given the context in which they work. For example, a teacher who early in the year gets a firm grip of a boy and strongly implies physical aggression if he does not settle down, may quite genuinely have the child's academic achievement in mind, believing that the child will work well in response to 'firm treatment'.

Similarly, the teacher who relinquishes an authoritarian role and digresses from the syllabus in order to suit the interests of the pupils may regard it as the teacher's responsibility to improve the quality of the classroom environment, to attempt to deal with the feelings of resentment that pupils have for school and authority and to provide them with more satisfying school experiences. Whether or not we regard these as survival strategies depends upon how broadly or narrowly we wish to conceptualise teaching. One might equally well interpret these strategies (or at least, some of them) as the classroom skills of the urban school teacher. Just as the recitation in some contexts may fulfil a useful teaching function, Woods's survival strategies may help teachers to motivate and instruct their pupils, given the context in which they find themselves.

Nevertheless, Woods's study does raise the issue of what constraints teachers should be expected to cope with and what kinds of strategies they should adopt in response. Certainly, the nature of schooling and the role of teachers has changed radically over recent years. Hargreaves (1982) for example, points out how schools now generally have much less support from the local community than they did, and how the attitudes of pupils as well as parents towards school have changed. In addition, there are many new demands placed upon education. Schools are commonly expected to provide a preparation for life and for a technologically oriented future, for instance, as well as fulfilling the traditionally accepted functions of developing basic skills and knowledge and encouraging appropriate standards of behaviour. The demands upon schools, and upon teachers, have certainly increased and are increasing. Within this debate about what schools are for and what is to be expected of our teachers, teachers themselves inevitably have a useful contribution to make.

CONSTRAINTS AND IDENTITIES

It has sometimes been argued that since teachers' and pupils' classroom behaviour is shaped by various constraints, both teachers and pupils find themselves thrust into fulfilling particular roles within the classroom. In addition, since teachers and pupils spend a considerable amount of time in classrooms, constant reaffirmation of these roles affects how they come to think of themselves, their own self-concepts and identities.

Certainly, beginning teachers seem to feel 'forced' into an authoritarian teacher role when they first enter schools. Expectations from pupils, teachers and most of all, the headteacher, are quite clearly communicated in interactions within the school. Beginning teachers may feel reluctant about accepting this role, but nevertheless find themselves adopting it.

Studies of teachers' perceptions of pupils also demonstrate a common repertoire of stereotyped roles that teachers assign to pupils – the 'troublemaker', the 'class clown', the 'boisterous boys', the 'quiet, intelligent girls' (see Calderhead 1981). Again, it is possible that some of these labels emerge as a result of the tasks and the context of the classroom. Denscombe (1980), for example, suggests that noisy talkative pupils are more readily labelled as deviant than quieter children, because the need to control noise is a prominent constraint. Noise coming from a classroom – particularly pupil-initiated noise – is generally interpreted within schools as reflecting the competence of the teacher, and teachers are therefore keen to keep the noise levels in their classrooms to a minimum. Denscombe suggests that in consequence, noisy pupils can become labelled as deviant even though their deviance is of a relatively minor nature.

Pupils have also been found to acquire stereotyped perceptions of themselves and their peers, according to their responses to the school context. Studies by Hargreaves (1967), Lacey (1970) and Woods (1979) in secondary schools indicate how pupils become increasingly polarised in their values and attitudes towards school as they progress through it. Those who succeed at school generally conform to its values since it is in their interest to do so, but those who do not succeed sometimes adopt anti-school attitudes and develop values which are antagonistic to the school. It is suggested that an anti-school sub-culture allows those who fail at school to experience achievement in deviance, and acquire a more positive identity through commitment to its alternative values.

Although there is some persuasive evidence that the constraints of the institution affect the nature of the interactions among teachers and pupils and the ways in which they may come to perceive themselves and each other, it is inevitable that individuals will in fact negotiate different roles with different impact upon their self-perceptions. The processes involved are undoubtedly complex and not easily disentangled, although it may well be of value for teachers to be aware of some of the possible interrelationships.

IMPLICATIONS FOR TEACHERS

While teachers may often express discontent or uneasiness about schools and about teaching, they typically accept the school context as given and view their job as working within the constraints that exist. Issues concerning what education is for, or how science ought to be taught, for example, are often regarded as someone else's responsibility. However, if teachers are to exert greater control over the nature of their classroom practice, they may have to come to a fuller understanding of the wider context in which their practice has developed. They may have to heighten their awareness of the influences and constraints that contribute to the framework within which they make their own individual decisions, so that they realise both the potential and the limitations of their own actions. Research on classrooms and ethnographic studies of teaching may have an important role to play in this respect. By sensitising teachers to the effects of certain influences and constraints – how they shape classroom practice, determine the degree of success of certain innovations, and contribute to certain roles and relationships within the classroom – they can encourage and direct teachers to a critical reflection upon their own circumstances. Such reflection might enable teachers to become more constructively involved in determining their own classroom practice.

RECOMMENDED READING

Kelly, A.V. (1980) *Curriculum Context*. London: Harper and Row.
   A collection of papers, each examining different types of influences upon the school curriculum.
Lacey, C. (1977) *The Socialisation of Teachers*. London: Methuen.
   Examines the nature of teacher socialisation and reports a series of case studies on student teachers' transition into the role of teacher.
Sharp, R. and Green, A. (1975) *Education and Social Control: a Study in Progressive Primary Education*. London: Routledge and Kegan Paul.
   A controversial book which attempts to relate classroom processes to the wider functioning of schools within society. Much of the book focuses upon interviews with three teachers and their pupils in a London primary school.
Woods, P. (1979) *The Divided School*. London: Routledge and Kegan Paul.
   An ethnographic study of a secondary modern school in the Midlands. Woods reports the strategies adopted by teachers and pupils in order to survive the institutional context of the school.

EXERCISES

1.   While observing another teacher, identify those strategies whose main function appears to be to cope with the classroom context. Discuss these strategies with the teacher afterwards. To what extent does the teacher's account support your interpretation?

2. List six areas of school policy, or six different school rules which affect teachers' practice (e.g. concerning the marking of work, conduct in the school, etc.). Why have these policies or rules come about? What influences and constraints might have shaped their development?

3. Considering Lacey's three strategies for adapting to institutional pressures (strategic redefinition, strategic compliance, and internalised adjustment), list instances of each strategy from your own experience. What factors might determine which strategy you adopted in moving to a new school?

4. While observing teachers in class or small-group teaching, identify periods of recitation. Describe the functions you think these recitations are fulfilling. Match your interpretations against those of the teacher.

5. Examine one lesson that you have planned and taught. List those constraints that in some way influenced your planning and classroom interaction. Over which of these factors could you exert some control?

6

Learning to Teach

THE FIRST DAZE OF TEACHING

WHEN newly qualified teachers take up their first appointments, their initial experiences in school are often accompanied by a mixture of interest, enthusiasm, considerable anxiety and confusion. The first few days in particular, when they meet new colleagues and pupils and suddenly face the demands of being fully responsible for a class, commonly result in feelings of stress and mental exhaustion. The fact that many new teachers feel ill-equipped for the task before them and that feelings of competence can sometimes take a long time to develop, raises a number of interesting questions about how teachers learn to teach, how beginning teachers adjust to classroom life and how this adjustment might be more easily achieved.

RESEARCH ON THE EXPERIENCES OF BEGINNING TEACHERS

Research into the attitudes, opinions and experiences of teachers, particularly during the period of transition from student to teacher, outlines a number of difficulties in learning to teach. Fuller, for example, conducted several interview and questionnaire studies to investigate the concerns of primary school teachers at different stages in their careers (Fuller 1969, Fuller and Bown 1975). Three phases are suggested, each characterised by different types of concern. Not all teachers progress through these phases in the same way or at the same rate, but the suggested developmental pattern is a fairly typical one.

Firstly, in the *pre-teaching phase*, the period before student teachers have had any extensive contact with class teaching, prospective teachers' concerns are largely unformulated. Although they may experience some anxiety about entering the classroom, this anxiety is not focused upon any particular problems. Teaching does not appear to be viewed as a particularly difficult or troublesome task. It would seem that beginning teachers early in their career are not really aware of the demands about to be made upon them. The *early teaching phase* starts at the first substantial contact beginning teachers have with a class, and generally extends through the first two years of full time teaching. This phase is characterised by concerns with their own professional competence. Beginning teachers are anxious about whether they are doing the 'right thing', and are particularly concerned about their ability to manage and control the class. This is followed by the *late teaching phase* in which concern shifts from self to pupils. Teachers, at this stage, appear to be mostly concerned with pupils' attainment, pupils' learning and the quality of their educational experience. Teachers are still concerned about improving their teaching performance, but the concern is no longer one of questioning their own competence but of deciding how changes in their teaching might lead to improved learning on the part of the pupils.

Taylor (1975) reported similar evidence from an investigation of the concerns of beginning secondary school teachers. At the completion of their training the teachers were provided with a list of forty concerns, each with a 1 to 5 scale, ranging from 'of no concern' to 'of very considerable concern'. The teachers were instructed first to reflect back on their experiences at the beginning of their teacher training course and to record their level of concern at that time, and second to record their level of concern at present. Taylor found that the greatest concerns related to self-adequacy and the ability to control the class – those of Fuller's *early teaching phase*. These were rated highly in both sets of ratings, although the level of concern was reported to be slightly less at the end of the course than at the beginning.

Some researchers have suggested that there may be a fourth phase of teacher concerns which occurs after about seven years of teaching and is characterised by feelings of frustration and disillusionment and is accompanied by doubts which relate more to the wider teaching profession than to personal competence (see Schwab and Iwanicki 1982). This phase – sometimes termed 'teacher burn-out' – is probably as deserving of attention as the earlier ones. Certainly, teachers commonly report feeling 'stale' and 'unchallenged', particularly after several years in the same school, and one could well expect this to influence the quality of their classroom teaching. Although some teachers may seek a psychological release or fresh stimulus by changing schools or obtaining secondment to an advanced training course, it is all too obvious in some staffrooms that many teachers have resolved simply to live with the problem.

Taylor suggests that the concerns of teachers particularly during the period of initial training have important implications for teacher training itself. He argues that much of the teacher training curriculum is unrelated to the concerns and difficulties of beginning teachers, and is therefore likely to be perceived by teachers themselves as largely irrelevant. He further claims that teacher training generally has taken far too little account of helping beginning teachers cope with classroom difficulties. Such claims find considerable support amongst students and teachers. Surveys of teachers' opinions on their teacher training typically reveal that they find very little of their training to be applicable in their professional lives. Areas of the teacher training curriculum such as sociology, psychology and curriculum theory are in particular reported to be unhelpful. Not surprisingly the most valued aspects tend to be those related directly to classroom practice, particularly experience in schools (see Morrison and McIntyre 1973, Her Majesty's Inspectorate 1982).

Parallel to the early changes in teachers' concerns, *teachers' attitudes and opinions about teaching* also tend to change. As discussed in Chapter 5, before entry to teacher training, students generally have fairly traditional attitudes to teaching and to authority. Teacher training then appears to have a 'liberalising' effect, resulting in students' attitudes becoming more child-centred. After training, however, they revert to the 'latent culture' (Lacey 1976, Tabachnick et al. 1982) and new teachers adopt the more authoritarian, control-oriented beliefs and attitudes that they used to hold before their teacher training began. These changes in attitude are often accompanied by some difficulties in adjusting to the life of the school, and coming to share its values.

The changes in beginning teachers' concerns and attitudes and the difficulties they experience in adjusting to the values, beliefs and practices of the school are probably not unconnected. Beginning teachers approach teaching with certain expectations of what classroom life will be like. They have certain beliefs about teaching and the kind of teacher they would like to be. For a few teachers their expectations may come fairly close to reality. In consequence, they may feel able to cope and the adjustment to classroom life may be made quite easily. For others, however, neither their expectations for classrooms nor the expectations they have for their own teaching meet the reality they perceive. For these, the transition from student to teacher can be quite alarming and is typically accompanied by numerous self-doubts. When it is evident that their practices cannot be implemented as expected and that there is great difficulty in becoming the kind of teacher they want to be, beginning teachers may feel they have no alternative but to adopt the practice which can be readily seen to work and with which, as pupils, they were familiar. This change in practice may not so much reflect a desire for conformity on the part of the novice, as their inability to establish an alternative. A change to the practice that 'works' is also likely to be accompanied by a change in attitudes about teaching, and possibly the development of a rationalisation to justify the position. This is typified in the comment of a middle school teacher, interviewed by Pollard (1980):

> I start off trying to be child-centred and doing all the stuff that they teach you at college. I still believe in that but it's very hard to do when you have not got much equipment and the kids aren't used to it, so I've compromised quite a lot. (p. 38.)

The transition from student to teacher, variously labelled *culture shock* (Evans 1976) or *transition shock* (Corcoran 1981), is clearly an uneasy one for many teachers and is an obvious source of concern for those involved in training teachers. Research into the nature of teachers' difficulties in learning to teach seems to imply that teacher training would be more helpful and effective if it was more relevant to the experiences of teachers and offered more support in helping teachers to develop or change their classroom practice in a school context.

THE TRAINING OF TEACHERS

The initial training of teachers has generally come to be structured around four main components: *subject studies*, such as mathematics or English, which provide teachers with an academic knowledge base; *methods courses*, which deal with the teaching of subjects in schools and introduce students to the materials and methods in use; *educational studies*, which include psychological, sociological and curriculum theory contributions to the understanding of educational issues; and *teaching practice*, in which students engage in supervised teaching within schools. This training is spread over three or four years in the case of BEd courses. In the case of one-year postgraduate courses it is assumed that the academic component has been covered in the student's first degree, and the training focuses upon the methods, educational studies and practice components.

Opinions as to what is an appropriate form of training, and how much emphasis should be placed upon each component have varied somewhat, and teacher training courses in Britain have for a long time been characterised by some diversity. In general, however, training courses have, for at least the past decade, mostly been based upon a philosophy of *teacher education* as opposed to *teacher training*, the distinction being that the former is concerned with producing a knowledgeable, well-educated teacher as opposed to a classroom practitioner or 'technician' (see Hirst 1976). While many would still agree that teachers should be knowledgeable in the subject matter they teach and possess an understanding of educational issues, and therefore be able to make well-informed judgements when faced with educational problems, it is also obviously important that teachers acquire the more precise skills of classroom practice. An emphasis on teacher *education* may, however, have contributed to the development of courses which were academic in orientation at the expense of the more practical aspects of teaching and the skills of the classroom.

In contrast, recent years have seen a steadily increasing demand for teachers to possess a range of sophisticated classroom skills. Increases in school indiscipline, growing numbers of ethnic minorities in the classroom, innovations such as open-plan schools, mixed ability teaching, and team-teaching, and the growth of the pastoral care function of school all require the teacher to develop new skills. The number of areas in which it might be hoped that teachers develop at least minimal competence is now in fact so great that, given the time available for initial training, even those courses well-oriented to the development of classroom skills have inevitably to be selective in those they choose to promote.

Not surprisingly, there is a heightened concern amongst teacher educators about the nature and appropriateness of courses of initial training. A survey of probationer teachers carried out by HMI (1982) estimated that as many as a quarter of all new teachers were inadequately prepared for the classroom. The findings of this survey have stimulated a number of recommendations for the restructuring of teacher training courses (DES 1983). In particular, it is suggested that teacher training should become oriented more towards professional practice, involve more time in schools, and focus to a greater extent upon developing the knowledge and skills that students will require in the classroom. However, this raises a number of questions. What knowledge and skills do teachers require? How can these be developed in student teachers?

At this point, it is interesting to compare the nature of teacher training in Britain with that in the United States of America. Whereas the past decade or two of British teacher education has been strongly influenced by views of developing well-educated personnel, US teacher training has focused much more upon the development of skilled classroom practitioners. In the 1960s, teaching came to be popularly viewed as a collection of skills or competencies that could be identified and individually learned and practised and gradually assembled into a coherent and effective form of practice (see Gage and Winne 1975). This was a skills development approach to teacher training, generally referred to as *competency based teacher education* (CBTE). Various procedures were developed, some of which have been imported into a few British teacher training courses, to promote skill learning. Many of the skills on which these techniques have focused have been identified largely through reflection and common sense or from the findings of teacher effectiveness studies. By and large, the procedures have been developed far ahead of research on teaching and of our ability to understand the development, employment and effectiveness of teaching skills in the classroom.

One of the most widespread innovations in classroom skill training is *microteaching*. Originally developed at Stanford University in California, it was based on the principle of behaviour modification. Students would teach a brief lesson to a small group of pupils, focusing upon one of a series of listed skills (such as *varying the stimulus*, or *asking probing questions*). Before the lesson, the nature and function of the skill would be explained and it might also be demonstrated. Varying the stimulus, for example, would be explained as a skill intended to change the focus of children's attention quite frequently with the aim of maintaining interest and involvement. The lesson itself would be videotaped and immediately afterwards replayed to the student who would receive feedback from a tutor about her or his performance of the skill. The student would then be given some time to consider how to improve the lesson before re-teaching it to another small group of pupils and once again discussing performance (see Allen and Ryan 1969, Brown 1975).

The original microteaching programme has since been adapted in various ways. The programme at Stirling University for example, (see McIntyre, MacLeod and Griffiths 1977) employs a series of observation schedules to provide more explicit feedback on the use of particular skills. When students practise varying the stimulus, for instance, they will generally be observed by some of their peers who note on a coding form every 30 seconds whether they were engaged in movement, gesture, changing the mode of speech, or changing the focus of pupil attention, and also whether pupils were talking and moving. At the end of the lesson the codings of the students' behaviour are then used to consider how successfully the students varied the stimulus and to help

point out those aspects of teaching behaviour that require modification
if the students are to be more effective in arousing and maintaining pupil
interest. Some microteaching programmes have involved demonstration
videotapes of the skills to be developed, and others incorporate
microteaching within a more general course of study of teaching skills,
involving the analysis of lesson transcripts and more detailed discussion
of the nature and appropriateness of the defined skills (e.g. Borg and
Stone 1974).

A number of arguments have been put both for and against the use of
microteaching. It has been argued that microteaching provides a safe
training opportunity in which students have a greater chance to
concentrate on the development of classroom skills, to obtain specific
feedback about their teaching competence and to build up confidence
before entering a normal classroom. MacLeod and McIntyre (1977)
argue that microteaching does help to change the ways in which students
think about their teaching and enables them to develop routines which
can later be transferred to classroom practice. On the other hand, critics
of microteaching have argued that it focuses on a fairly narrow range of
skills and it has not been clearly demonstrated to lead to more
competent teaching than conventional training, and therefore does not
warrant the extra costs in terms of equipment and staff.

Certainly, problems have frequently been found in transferring the
skills learned in microteaching to the reality of a classroom setting (see
Joyce, Brown and Peck 1981, Copeland 1981). Joyce, for example,
points out how teachers can frequently demonstrate skills in a
laboratory setting yet do not incorporate the same skills into their
teaching in the classroom. Joyce suggests that in the more complex
environment of the classroom, teachers have little opportunity to
employ the skills they have learned in the teaching laboratory. It is
suggested that the skills demanded in the task of instructing a class of
thirty, where management concerns also become pressing, are different
from those needed for small group instruction. Some microteaching
programmes, however, attempt to improve the level of transfer between
the laboratory and the classroom by the use of link-experiences, such as
teaching a class of twenty a 20–30 minute lesson in a microteaching
context which is designed to integrate skills developed in previous small
group sessions. The aim is to provide students with a more classroom-
like environment in which to practise and integrate learned skills before
taking them into real classrooms, although its effectiveness in achieving
these aims is unknown. Copeland argues that the real classroom
environment is inevitably different from the environment of the
laboratory, and when beginning teachers go into schools, they learn a
whole new set of skills with which to cope. To support this case, he

quotes an illuminating example of the impact of the classroom environment on two students' management strategies.

The students, on different teaching practice placements, were observed to adopt markedly different strategies for controlling classroom behaviour. One was quietly spoken, rewarded conforming behaviour and achieved a good relationship with the pupils. The other engaged in a good deal of shouting, achieved control through threat and coercion and did not appear to have established a very satisfactory rapport with the children. However, when the two students exchanged classes, their teaching approaches also changed.The quietly spoken one engaged in more shouting and came to rely more on threat and coercion for maintaining control, whereas the other student became more quietly spoken, started to reward good behaviour and establish a more pleasant relationship with the children. Copeland reckons that pupils have become used to reacting to teachers in particular ways and that this style of reacting is a powerful force in moulding beginning teachers' strategies. Copeland suggests that beginning teachers learn to adopt those strategies that 'work' and what 'works' depends to a large extent upon the kind of teaching the pupils are used to. The implication for microteaching – or in fact any form of training in teaching skills – is that attention must be paid to the context in which teachers develop and extend their classroom skills. Either the contexts which beginning teachers first meet and in which they develop their classroom practice must be carefully selected so as to enable them to use their learned skills and for them to be reinforced and extended, or the nature of their training must be expanded to provide them with a greater range of skills from which students can select those appropriate for the classroom environments they face.

If microteaching does not cue students in to the features that are most appropriate for them to notice in a real classroom setting it may have little lasting constructive effect.

Simulation is another technique that has been applied and developed in teacher training. In its simplest form this has taken the form of critical incident training. Similar to the in-basket techniques commonly used in management training, critical incident training involves the resolution of hypothetical teaching situations, either by students on their own, or more often in discussion with other students and a tutor. Situations such as

> You are taking a class for games. Janet has brought a note saying she has a cold and cannot take part. You ask her to sit along the edge of the gym and watch. Soon you notice she is deriding the efforts of people in the class, some of whom are irritated, some amused by her comments. You ask her to cease but later she does the same thing again. (Wragg 1981, p. 20)

will be used to provoke thought about appropriate teaching strategies and to consider how different responses could be justified. Several textbooks for teachers include some incidents for this purpose, or provide extensive lists of possible classroom incidents to which teachers may be called upon to respond (Corsini and Howard 1964, Bishop and Whitfield 1973).

Such incidents may encourage students to think about certain classroom difficulties in advance, to consider the information they might need to take into account, and to develop alternative ideas on how to respond. However, the technique also has limitations. As with microteaching, unless the problems considered are ones which occur soon afterwards in the students' experience in classrooms, and unless they are similar to problems encountered in classroom life, the value of critical incident training may well be lost. In addition, discussion of large numbers of critical incidents and different possible solutions might, when students have little experience to relate the discussion, lead to more confusion than clarification.

More elaborate simulation exercises involve the use of hypothetical school records and databanks of information about pupils which can be consulted in deciding how to cope with an array of particular problems (Marsh 1979). Some simulations involve role-play in which students act out a response to an incident, and fellow students may act the parts of the pupils. Technological versions have involved the use of film or videotape to present classroom problems for discussion, and in some cases provide videotaped 'reactions' to alternative treatments. Twelker (1967), for example, developed a simulation in which students were given background information about a hypothetical school and on each of the pupils in one of its classes. A film presented 20 classroom incidents occurring throughout the school day. After each incident a student would act out a response, and a tutor would select one of four possible filmed reactions, according to which reaction the tutor felt to be most appropriate. Megarry (1980) describes more recent computerised attempts to present similar interactive simulations.

Teaching skills workbooks have also recently been developed to provide information and practice exercises for teachers to use in the development of particular skills. Evertson et al. (1981) developed a skills workbook on classroom management based upon their research on management in the primary school. The workbook presents activities aimed to develop those skills identified in research as used by effective managers. It provides checklists of the type of planning decisions made by effective managers, and the kinds of classroom rules that effective teachers employed, and the strategies they adopted for monitoring classroom behaviour or preventing inappropriate behaviour. The aim of these materials is not to recommend one style of effective teaching, but to describe a range of teaching practices from which beginning teachers may be able to select and adapt those which appear useful and which can be incorporated into their own teaching style. A similar series of teaching skills workbooks for secondary school teaching has been produced by the Teacher Education Project, based at Nottingham, Leicester and Exeter universities (e.g. Wragg 1981, Kerry 1982). Each workbook focuses on a particular aspect of teaching practice, such as questioning, explaining or classroom management. They present a series of tasks for teachers and students to perform, including observational tasks in classrooms, analysing classroom transcripts and critical incidents to provoke thought and discussion. They also provide brief summaries of the findings of classroom research and checklists of the types of behaviours that experienced teachers have been observed to adopt in the classroom. The OU (1979) Curriculum in Action materials also aim to provide teachers with exercises to focus their attention on the processes at work in their own classrooms, although they do not emphasise the development of particular skills. Barnes (1982) has developed a workbook focusing on the tasks involved in curriculum development. Little evaluation has so far been conducted on the use of these materials, although Emmer et al. (1981) carried out an experimental study in in-service training using Evertson's classroom management workbook. Twenty-three teachers were provided with the manual before the beginning of the school year. They also took part in two workshop sessions in which management skills were discussed and videotapes were used to demonstrate particular skills in action. Observation of these in-service teachers in the classroom revealed that they succeeded in implementing many of the suggested strategies and obtained significantly higher levels of pupil task engagement and appropriate behaviour than a control group of teachers who were matched in terms of years of experience and the age of pupils taught. Later, in the middle of the school year, half of the control group were also given the management workbook and the workshop experiences, but this training had much less impact than that given to the larger group at the beginning of the year. Having established a style of classroom management with a particular class, teachers found it difficult, and were perhaps also less motivated, to make any substantial change.

Skills training procedures have generally been developed far ahead of our ability to understand teachers' practice and its development. Their development has often been guided by common sense, evaluations of their effects have been relatively few, and the conclusions of these evaluations often contradictory. It is only with the recent increased number of investigations into teachers' and student teachers' thinking and decision-making that a satisfactory explanation has been achieved concerning how certain forms of skill training might facilitate the development of teachers' classroom practice.

Beginning teachers, it has been found, generally have fairly simple, unsophisticated means of interpreting the classroom environment and their own practice within it. Research on student teachers' planning, for example (Joyce and Harootunian 1964, Ben-Peretz 1981) suggests that students' plans are generally crude and lacking in detail and appear to be based on students' observations of more experienced teachers. Student teachers lack any extensive knowledge of pupils, curricular materials and appropriate forms of classroom organisation and are therefore hampered in the process of designing activities that will be manageable and instructionally effective. Experienced teachers, on the other hand, are often able to predict pupil responses to particular material or activities (Leinhardt and Seewald 1981, Calderhead 1983) and have much clearer and more detailed conceptions than novices of what their pupils know and how they approach activities (Leinhardt 1982). Experienced teachers also appear to have an extensive memorised repertoire of activities – 'plans in memory' – which are readily implemented in the classroom.

During classroom interaction it would seem that experienced teachers have learned to be attuned to certain cues which signal, for example, pupils' attention, work rate, and understanding. They respond to these cues in various and complex ways, often combining both management and instruction in their teaching strategies. In contrast, Copeland (1981) suggests that to the novice teacher the classroom presents a 'bewildering kaleidoscope of people, behaviour, events and interactions only dimly understood' (p. 11). The rapidity, variety and complexity of classroom behaviour, often fulfilling multiple functions, is not easily tuned in to or comprehended. With an unsophisticated means of interpreting classroom processes, beginning teachers not surprisingly have difficulty in guiding their classroom practice.

In learning to teach, beginning teachers have to acquire considerable knowledge about pupils, about the materials in use, the subject matter and the curricular context, and about appropriate forms of classroom organisation. They also have to acquire skills of cueing in to relevant information as they teach, and interpreting and acting upon these cues. Much of this learning has in the past been left to trial and error. Teachers have largely acquired their classroom skills through their own experience in the classroom aided perhaps by the occasional discussion with a tutor or fellow teacher. The challenge that presently faces teacher education is how these areas of knowledge and skill can be more systematically presented to beginning teachers to develop their teaching practice. Certainly, many of the skills-training techniques mentioned above help to make students more aware of the knowledge required in teaching, and some of them have the potential to help beginning teachers to develop ways of interpreting classroom events and thinking about their own teaching which might guide their practice in the classroom.

At the same time, some techniques may be less than efficient training devices. Being too removed from the real-life classroom situation they may only encourage students to think about their teaching in ways which will later have to be abandoned. Continued experimentation with these techniques, however, given an understanding of how they affect the development of student teachers' practice, might enable teacher education to rise to the current challenge.

THE ROLE OF RESEARCH IN TEACHER EDUCATION

Educational research is often viewed by teachers as unhelpful, unnecessary and unrelated to the everyday practice of teaching. Much educational research may indeed be irrelevant to teachers' work, but this view of research may also be partly due to some unrealistic expectations. It is often assumed, for example, that in order for research to be helpful to teachers it must provide ready solutions to classroom problems. However, there are many reasons why research could not fulfil such a role. First, classroom processes are complex and often unpredictable. Generalisations about the solutions to particular problems or the effects of particular teaching actions cannot take account of the unique qualities of each classroom and each teaching situation. Because of the varied contexts in which teachers work, situations may present themselves differently, and demand quite different responses. Second, teachers themselves bring their own values and beliefs to teaching which inevitably predispose them to the selection of particular strategies and the seeking of particular outcomes.

A more feasible and productive role for educational research is in providing the conceptual means by which teachers can reflect upon their own and others' teaching and consider how it can be changed and developed. McIntyre (1980), for example, suggests that the contribution of research to teacher quality lies in its potential to reveal the nature of classroom practice and to allow its critical scrutiny in the context of teacher training and professional development.

Research on teachers' thinking and decision-making certainly fulfils this role, providing us with a way of conceptualising teachers' practice, and revealing the kinds of knowledge that teachers have acquired, the interpretations they make of classroom events and how these guide teachers' actions. The value of this research is not in providing prescriptions for practice or recipes for teaching, but in helping teachers to acquire a better understanding of the nature of their practice, how it has developed, how it is influenced and constrained by the context in which they work, and how it influences pupils' learning and attitudes. To beginning teachers faced with the task of acquiring classroom skills, and to more experienced teachers facing the demands of new curricula, social conditions and school organisation, research can assist in their continuous efforts to analyse, appraise and reconstruct their own practice. In addition, if teachers accept the value of research, they may come to take a more active involvement in the process itself, identifying issues which require fuller investigation and contributing towards a form of research which is practical, relevant and useful in their own professional development.

Bibliography

Allen, D. & Ryan, K. (1969) *Microteaching*. Reading, Massachusetts: Addison-Wesley.

Anderson, L.M. (1982) 'Short-term student responses to classroom instruction'. *The Elementary School Journal*, **82**, 97–108.

Anderson, L.M. & Brubaker, N.L. (1983) 'Students doing seatwork: patterns of adequate and poor responses'. Research report of the Institute for Research on Teaching, University of Michigan, East Lansing.

Anderson, L.M., Evertson, C.M. & Emmer, E.T. (1980) 'Dimensions in classroom management derived from recent research'. *Journal of Curriculum Studies*, **12**, 343–56.

Armstrong, M. (1980) *Closely Observed Children*. London: Writers and Readers.

Ashton, P., Kneen, P., Davies, F. & Holley, B.J. (1975) *The Aims of Primary Education: a study of teachers' opinions*. London: Macmillan.

Aston, A. (1980) 'The humanities curriculum project'. In Stenhouse, L. (ed.) *Curriculum Research and Development in Action*. London: Heinemann Educational.

Ball, S.J. (1981) *Beachside Comprehensive: a case study of secondary schooling*. Cambridge: Cambridge University Press.

Barnes, D. (1982) *Practical Curriculum Study*. London: Routledge and Kegan Paul.

Bennett, S.N. & Desforges, C.W. (1984) *The Quality of Pupil Learning*. London: Lawrence Erlbaum.

Ben-Peretz, M. (1981) 'The form and substance of teachers' lesson planning'. Paper presented at the American Educational Research Association, Los Angeles, California, 1981.

Ben-Peretz, M. & Tamir, P. (1981) 'What teachers want to know about curriculum materials'. *Journal of Curriculum Studies*, **13**, 45–54.

Bishop, A.J. & Whitfield, R.C. (1972) *Situations in Teaching*. London: McGraw-Hill.

Bliss, I. (1976) 'Language use in contrasting schools'. Unpublished MEd thesis, University of Leicester.

Bloom, B.S. (1976) *Human Characteristics and School Learning*. New York: McGraw-Hill.

Borg, W.R. & Ascione, F.R. (1982) Classroom management in elementary mainstreaming classrooms. *Journal of Educational Psychology*, **74**, 85–95.

Borg, W.R. & Stone, D.R. (1974) Protocol materials as a tool for changing teacher behaviour. *Journal of Experimental Education*, **43**(1), 34–9.

Borko, H., Shavelson, R.J. & Stern, P. (1981) 'Teachers' decisions in the planning of reading instruction'. *Reading Research Quarterly*, **16**, 449–66.

Bossert, S.T. (1979) *Tasks and Social Relationships in Classrooms*. Cambridge: Cambridge University Press.

Bredo, E. (1980) 'Contextual influences on teachers' instructional approaches'. *Journal of Curriculum Studies*, **12**.

Brophy, J. (1981) 'Teacher praise: a functional analysis'. *Review of Educational Research*, **51**, 5–33.

Brophy, J.E. & Good, T.L. (1974) *Teacher-Student Relationships*: *Causes and Consequences*. New York: Holt, Rinehart and Winston.

Brown, G. (1975) *Microteaching*: *a Programme of Teaching Skills*. London: Methuen.

Brown, S. & McIntyre, D. (1982) 'Costs and rewards of innovation: taking account of the teachers' viewpoint'. In Olson, J. (ed.) *Innovation in the Science Curriculum*. London: Croom Helm.

Calderhead, J. (1979) 'Teachers' classroom decision-making: its relationship to teachers' perceptions of pupils and to classroom interaction'. Unpublished PhD thesis, University of Stirling.

Calderhead, J. (1981) 'A psychological approach to research on teachers' classroom decision-making'. *British Educational Research Journal*, **7**, 51–7.

Calderhead, J. (1983) 'Research into teachers' and student teachers' cognitions: exploring the nature of classroom practice'. Paper presented at the American Educational Research Association, Montreal, 1983.

Clark, C.M. & Elmore, J.L. (1981) 'Transforming curriculum in mathematics, science and writing: a case study of teacher yearly planning'. Research report of the Institute for Research on Teaching, University of Michigan, East Lansing.

Clark, C.M. & Yinger, R.J. (1979) 'Teachers' thinking'. In Peterson, P.L. & Walberg, H.J. (eds) *Research on Teaching*: *concepts, findings and implications*. Berkeley, California: McCutchan.

Clark, C.M. & Yinger, R.J. (1980) 'The hidden world of teaching'. Research report of the Institute for Research on Teaching, University of Michigan, East Lansing.

Cohen, L. & Manion, L. (1981) *Perspectives on Classrooms and Schools*. Eastbourne: Holt, Rinehart and Winston.

Cooper, H. & Good, T. (1983) *Pygmalion Grows Up*: *Studies in the expectation communication process*. New York: Academic Press.

Copeland, W.D. (1981) 'Clinical experiences in the education of teachers'. *Journal of Education for Teaching*, **7**, 3–17.

Corcoran, E. (1981) 'Transition shock: the beginning teacher's paradox'. *Journal of Teacher Education*, **32**(3), 19–23.

Corsini, R.J. & Howard, D.D. (1964) *Critical Incidents in Teaching*. Englewood Cliffs, New Jersey: Prentice-Hall.

deCharms, R. (1983) 'Intrinsic motivation, peer tutoring and co-operative learning: practical maxims'. In Levine, J.M. & Wang, M.C. (eds) *Teacher and Student Perceptions*: *Implications for Learning*. Hillsdale, New Jersey: Lawrence Erlbaum.

Deem, R. (1978) *Women and Schooling*. London: Routledge and Kegan Paul.
Denscombe, M. (1980) '"Keeping 'em quiet"': the significance of noise for the practical activity of teaching'. In Woods, P. (ed.) *Teacher Strategies*. London: Croom Helm.
Department of Education and Science (1983) *Teaching Quality*. London: Her Majesty's Stationery Office.
Docking, J.W. (1980) *Control and Discipline in Schools: Perspectives and Approaches*. London: Harper and Row.
Doyle, W. (1977) 'Paradigms for research on teacher effectiveness'. In Shulman, L. (ed.) *Review of Research in Education*, 5.
Doyle, W. (1979) 'Making managerial decisions in classrooms'. In Duke, D.L. (ed.) *Classroom Management*. 78th yearbook of the National Society for the Study of Education (part 2). Illinois: University of Chicago Press.
Doyle, W. (1979) Classroom tasks and students' abilities. In Peterson, P.L. & Walberg, H.I. (eds) *Research on Teaching: Concepts, Findings and Implications*. Berkeley, California: McCutchan.
Doyle, W. & Ponder, G.A. (1977) 'The practicality ethic and teacher decision-making'. *Interchange*, **8**, 1–12.
Duke, D.L. & Meckel, A.M. (1979) 'Disciplinary roles in American schools'. *British Journal of Teacher Education*, **6**, 37–49.
Eisner, E.W. (1967) 'Educational objectives: help or hindrance?'. *School Review*, **75**, 250–66.
Elliott, J. (1980) 'Implications of classroom research for professional development'. In Hoyle, E. & Megarry, J. (eds) *World Yearbook of Education, 1980*. London: Kogan Page.
Emmer, E.T., Sanford, J.P., Evertson, C.M., Clements, B.S. & Martin, J. (1981) 'The classroom management improvement study: an experiment in elementary school classrooms'. Research report of the Research and Development Center for Teacher Education, University of Texas at Austin.
Erlwanger, S. (1975) 'Case studies of children's mathematics'. *Journal of Children's Mathematical Behavior*, **1**, 157–83.
Evans, N. (1976) *Transition to Teaching*. New York: Holt, Rinehart and Winston.
Evertson, C.M. & Emmer, E.T. (1982) 'Effective management at the beginning of the school year in junior high classes'. *Journal of Educational Psychology*, **74**, 485–98.
Evertson, C.M. & Hickman, R.C. (1981) 'Tasks of teaching classes of varied group composition'. Research report of the Research and Development Center for Teacher Education, University of Texas at Austin.
Evertson, C.M., Emmer, E.T., Clements, B.S., Sanford, J.P., Worsham, M.E. & Williams, E.L. (1981) *Organizing and Managing the Elementary School Classroom*. The Research and Development Center for Teacher Education, University of Texas at Austin.
Filby, N.N. & Barnett, B.J. (1982) 'Student perceptions of "better readers" in elementary classrooms'. *The Elementary School Journal*, **82**, 435–51.
Fisher, C.W., Berliner, D.C., Filby, N.N., Marliave, R., Cahen, L.S. & Dishaw, M.M. (1981) 'Teaching behaviors, ALT and student achievement: an overview'. *Journal of Classroom Interaction*, **17**, 2–15.
Flanders, N.A. (1970) *Analysing Teaching Behavior*. Reading, Massachusetts: Addison-Wesley.

Fuller, F.F. (1969) 'Concerns of teachers'. *American Educational Research Journal*, **6**, 207–26.

Fuller, F.F. & Bown, O.H. (1975) 'Becoming a teacher'. In Ryan, K. (ed.) *Teacher Education*. 74th yearbook of the National Society for the Study of Education. Illinois: University of Chicago Press.

Gage, N.L. & Winne, P.H. (1975) 'Performance-based teacher education'. In Ryan, K. (ed.) *Teacher Education*, 74th yearbook of the National Society for the Study of Education. Illinois: University of Chicago Press.

Galton, M., Simon, B. & Croll, P. (1980) *Inside the Primary Classroom*. London: Routledge and Kegan Paul.

Gretton, J. & Jackson, M. (1975) *William Tyndale – Collapse of a School or a System?* London: Allen and Unwin.

Hamilton, D. (1975) 'Handling innovation in the classroom: two Scottish examples'. In Reid, W.A. and Walker, D.F. (eds) *Case Studies in Curriculum Change*. London: Routledge and Kegan Paul.

Hanson, D. & Herrington, M. (1976) *From College to Classroom*: *the Probationary Year*. London: Routledge and Kegan Paul.

Hargreaves, D.H. (1979) 'A phenomenological approach to classroom decision-making'. In Eggleston, J. (ed.) *Teacher Decision-Making in the Classroom*. London: Routledge and Kegan Paul.

Hargreaves, D.H. (1982) *The Challenge for the Comprehensive School*: *Culture, Curriculum and Community*. London: Routledge and Kegan Paul.

Hargreaves, D.H., Hester, S.K. & Mellor, F.J. (1975) *Deviance in Classrooms*. London: Routledge and Kegan Paul.

Her Majesty's Inspectorate (1982) *The New Teacher in School*. London: HMSO.

Hirst, P. (1976) 'The PGCE course: its objectives and their nature'. *British Journal of Teacher Education*, **2**, 7–21.

Hobbs, A., Kleinberg, S.M. & Martin, P.J. (1979) 'Decision-making in primary schools'. *Research in Education*, **21**, 79–82.

Hoffman, J.V. & Kugle, C.L. (1982) 'A study of theoretical orientation to reading and its relationship to teacher verbal feedback during reading instruction'. *The Journal of Classroom Interaction*, **18**, 2–8.

Holt, J. (1969) *How Children Fail*. Harmondsworth: Penguin.

Jackson, P.W. (1968) *Life in Classrooms*. New York: Holt, Rinehart and Winston.

Joyce, B.R. & Harootunian, B. (1964) 'Teaching as problem-solving'. *Journal of Teacher Education*, **15**, 420–7.

Joyce, B.R., Brown, C.G. & Peck, L. (1981) *Flexibility in Teaching*. New York: Longman.

Kedar-Voivodas, G. & Tannenbaum, A. (1979) 'Teachers' attitudes toward young deviant children'. *Journal of Educational Psychology*, **71**, 800–08.

Kelly, A.V. (ed.) (1980) *Curriculum Context*. London: Harper and Row.

Kerry, T. (1982) *Effective Questioning*. London: Macmillan.

King, R. (1978) *All Things Bright and Beautiful?* Chichester: Wiley.

Kounin, J.S. (1970) *Discipline and Group Management in Classrooms*. New York: Holt, Rinehart and Winston.

Kulhavy, R.W. (1977) 'Feedback in written instruction'. *Review of Educational Research*, **47**, 211–32.

Lacey, C. (1977) *The Socialisation of Teachers*. London: Methuen.

Lawton, D. (1980) *The Politics of the School Curriculum*. London: Routledge and Kegan Paul.

Leinhardt, G. (1982) 'Expert and novice knowledge of individual student's achievement'. Paper presented at the American Educational Research Association conference, New York, 1982.

Leinhardt, G. & Seewald, A.M. (1981) 'Overlap: what's tested, what's taught?'. *Journal of Educational Measurement*, **18**, 85–96.

Lepper, M.R. (1983) 'Extrinsic reward and intrinsic motivation: implications for the classroom'. In Levine, J.M. & Wang, M.C. (eds) *Teacher and Student Perceptions: implications for learning*. Hillsdale, New Jersey: Lawrence Erlbaum.

Lundgren, U.P. (1974) 'Pedagogical roles in the classroom'. In Eggleston, J. (ed.) *Contemporary Research in the Sociology of Education*. London: Methuen.

McCuller, C.C. & Moseby, L.C. (1983) 'Disruptive and non-disruptive student perceptions of videotaped classroom simulations'. Research report of the Research and Development Center for Teacher Education, University of Texas at Austin.

McCutcheon, G. (1980) 'How do elementary school teachers plan? The nature of planning and influences on it'. *The Elementary School Journal*, **81**, 4–23.

McCutcheon, G. (1981) 'On the interpretation of classroom observations'. *Educational Researcher*, **10**, 5–10.

McIntyre, D. (1980) 'The contribution of research to quality in teacher education'. In Hoyle, E. & Megarry, J. (eds) *World Yearbook of Education*, 1980. London: Kogan Page.

McIntyre, D., MacLeod, G. & Griffiths, R. (1977) *Investigations into Microteaching*. London: Croom Helm.

Mackay, D.A. & Marland, P.W. (1978) 'Thought processes of teachers'. Paper presented at the American Educational Research Association, Toronto.

MacLeod, G. & McIntyre, D. (1977) 'Towards a model of microteaching'. *British Journal of Teacher Education*, **3**, 111–20.

McNair, K. & Joyce, B. (1979) 'Teachers' thoughts while teaching: the South Bay study, part 2'. Research report of the Institute of Research on Teaching, University of Michigan, East Lansing.

Marsh, C.J. (1979) 'Teacher education simulations: the challenge of change example'. *British Journal of Teacher Education*, **5**, 63–9.

Medley, D.M. (1979) 'The effectiveness of teachers'. In Peterson, P.L. & Walberg, H.J. (eds) *Research on Teaching: concepts, findings and implications*. Berkeley, California: McCutchan.

Medley, D.M. & Mitzel, H.E. (1963) 'Measuring classroom behavior by systematic observation'. In Gage, N.L. (ed.) *Handbook of Research on Teaching*. Chicago: Rand McNally.

Megarry, J. (1980) 'Selected innovations in methods of teacher education'. In Hoyle, E. & Megarry, J. *World Yearbook of Education, 1980*. London: Kogan Page.

Morine, G. (1976) 'A study of teacher planning'. Research report of the Far West Laboratory for Educational Research and Development, San Francisco, California.

Morine-Dershimer, G. (1979) 'Teacher conceptions of pupils – an outgrowth of instructional context: the South Bay study, part 3'. Research report of the Institute for Research on Teaching, University of Michigan, East Lansing.

Morine-Dershimer, G. (1982) 'Pupil perceptions of teacher praise'. *The Elementary School Journal*, **82**(5), 421–35.

Morrison, A. & McIntyre, D. (1973) *Teachers and Teaching* (2nd edn). London: Penguin.

Nash, R. (1973) *Classrooms Observed*. London: Routledge and Kegan Paul.

Olson, J. (1980) 'Teacher constructs and curriculum change'. *Journal of Curriculum Studies*, 12, 1–12.

Olson, J. (1982) 'Classroom knowledge and curriculum change'. In Olson, J. (ed.) *Innovation in the Science Curriculum*. London: Croom Helm.

Open University (1979) *Curriculum in Action*. Milton Keynes: Open University Press.

Partington, J.A. & Hinchliffe, G. (1979) 'Some aspects of classroom management'. *British Journal of Teacher Education*, 5, 231–41.

Peterson, P.L. & Clark, C.M. (1978) 'Teachers' reports of their cognitive processes during teaching'. *American Educational Research Journal*, 15, 555–65.

Peterson, P.L. & Swing, S.R. (1982) 'Beyond time on task: students' reports of their thought processes during classroom instruction'. *The Elementary School Journal*, 82(5), 481–93.

Peterson, P.L., Marx, R.W. & Clark, C.M. (1978) 'Teachers' planning, teacher behavior and student achievement'. *American Educational Research Journal*, 15, 417–32.

Pollard, A. (1980) 'Teacher interest and changing situations of survival threat in primary school classrooms'. In Woods, P. (ed.) *Teacher Strategies*. London: Croom Helm.

Prawat, R.S. (1980) 'Teacher perception of student affect'. *American Educational Research Journal*, 1, 61–75.

Rist, R.C. (1970) 'Student social class and teacher expectations: the self-fulfilling prophecy in ghetto education'. *Harvard Educational Review*, 40, 411–51.

Robertson, J. (1981) *Effective Classroom Control*. London: Hodder and Stoughton.

Rohrkemper, M.M. & Brophy, J.E. (1983) 'Teachers' thinking about problem students'. In Levine, J.M. & Wang, M.C. (eds) *Teacher and Student Perceptions: Implications For Learning*. Hillsdale, New Jersey: Lawrence Erlbaum.

Rosenshine, B.V. (1979) 'Content, time and direct instruction'. In Peterson, P.L. & Walberg, H.J. (eds) *Research on Teaching: Concepts, Findings and Implications*. Berkeley, California: McCutchan.

Ruddock, J. (1980) 'Insights into the process of dissemination'. *British Educational Research Journal*, 6, 139–47.

Saunders, M. (1979) *Class Control and Behavioural Problems*. London: McGraw-Hill.

Schwab, R.L. & Iwanicki, E.F. (1982) 'Perceived role conflict, role ambiguity and teacher burn-out'. *Educational Administration Quarterly*, 18, 60–74.

Sharp, R. & Green, A. (1975) *Education and Social Control*. London: Routledge and Kegan Paul.

Shavelson, R.J. (1973) 'What is the basic teaching skill?' *Journal of Teacher Education*, 24, 144–51.

Shipman, M.D. (1974) *Inside a Curriculum Project*. London: Methuen.

Silberman, C. (ed.) (1973) *The Open Classroom Reader*. New York: Random House.

Smith, L.C. & Geoffrey, W. (1968) *The Complexities of an Urban Classroom.* New York: Holt, Rinehart and Winston.

Snow, R.E. (1972) 'A model teacher training system: an overview'. Research report of the Stanford Center for Research and Development in Teaching, Stanford, California.

Stenhouse, L. (1970) *The Humanities Curriculum Project.* London: Heinemann.

Stenhouse, L. (1975) *An Introduction to Curriculum Research and Development.* London: Heinemann.

Stodolsky, S.S., Ferguson, T.L. & Wimpelberg, K. (1981) 'The recitation persists, but what does it look like?'. *Journal of Curriculum Studies,* **13,** 121–30.

Swing, S.R. & Peterson, P.L. (1982) 'The relationship of student ability and small-group interaction to student achievement'. *American Educational Research Journal,* **19,** 259–75.

Tabachnick, B.R., Zeichner, K.M., Densmore, K., Adler, S. & Egan, K. (1982) 'The impact of the student teaching experience on the development of teacher perspectives'. Paper presented at the American Educational Research Association Conference, New York, 1982.

Tattum, D. (1982) *Disruptive Pupils in Schools and Units.* Chichester: Wiley.

Taylor, P.H. (1970) *How Teachers Plan Their Courses.* London: National Foundation for Educational Research.

Taylor, P.H. (1974) *Purpose, Power and Constraint in the Primary School Curriculum.* London: Macmillan.

Taylor, P.H. (1975) 'A study of the concerns of students on a Postgraduate Certificate in Education course'. *British Journal of Teacher Education,* **1**(2), 151–61.

Twelker, P.A. (1967) 'Classroom simulation and teacher preparation'. *School Review,* **75,** 197–204.

Tyler, R.W. (1949) *Basic Principles of Curriculum and Instruction.* Chicago: University of Chicago Press.

Webb, N.M. (1982) 'Student interaction and learning in small groups'. *Review of Educational Research,* **52,** 421–46.

Westbury, I. (1980) 'Schooling as an agency of education: some implications for curriculum theory'. In Dockrell, W.B. & Hamilton, D. *Rethinking Educational Research,* London: Hodder and Stoughton.

Wheeler, D.K. (1967) *Curriculum Process.* London: University of London Press.

Winne, P.H. & Marx, R.W. (1977) 'Reconceptualizing research on teaching'. *Journal of Educational Psychology,* **69,** 668–78.

Winne, P.H. & Marx, R.W. (1982) 'Students' and teachers' views of thinking processes for classroom learning'. *The Elementary School Journal,* **92**(5), 493–519.

Woods, P. (1979) *The Divided School.* London: Routledge and Kegan Paul.

Worrall, C., Worrall, N. & Meldrum, C. (1983) 'The consequences of teacher praise and criticism'. *Educational Psychology,* **3,** 127–36.

Wragg, E.C. (1981) *Class Management and Control.* London: Macmillan.

Wragg, E.C. (ed.) (1983) *Classroom Teaching Skills.* London: Croom Helm.

Yinger, R.J. (1980) 'A study of teacher planning'. *The Elementary School Journal,* **80,** 107–27.

Zahorik, J.A. (1970) 'The effect of planning on teaching'. *The Elementary School Journal,* **71,** 143–51.

Zahorik, J.A. (1975) 'Teachers' planning models'. *Educational Leadership*, **33**, 134–9.

Zahorik, J.A. (1982) 'Learning activities: nature, function and practice'. *The Elementary School Journal*, **82**, 303–19.

Zeichner, K. & Tabachnick, B.R. (1981) 'Are the effects of university teacher education "washed out" by school experience?' *Journal of Teacher Education*, **32**, 7–11.

Name Index

Subject Index